SKEGNES
LIFEBOATS

AN ILLUSTRATED HISTORY

NICHOLAS LEACH

To the lifeboat crews of Skegness
past and present

Cover: Skegness lifeboats Lincolnshire Poacher and Leicester Fox II
at sea together off the town. (Nicholas Leach)

Title page: Skegness lifeboat Lincolnshire Poacher at speed.
(Nicholas Leach)

Published by
Landmark Publishing Ltd
Ashbourne Hall
Cokayne Avenue
Ashbourne
Derbyshire DE6 1EJ
England
Tel (01335) 347349 Fax (01335) 347303
landmark@clara.net
www.landmarkpublishing.co.uk

British Library Cataloguing in Publication Data.
A catalogue record for this book is available from the British Library.

ISBN 9781843064237

Layout by Nicholas Leach
Printed by Gutenberg Press, Malta

Contents

Introduction

Skegness stands on the Lincolnshire coast, north of the Wash and south of the Humber estuary. The seas offshore are characterised by shoals and sandbanks, many of which are between Skegness and the East Dudgeon lightship. From the Norfolk coast, a huge triangular area of shoal water, nearly twenty miles wide at its base, runs northwards for sixteen miles to the north-easterly point of the Docking Shoal, with its western edge almost forming an extension of the eastern shore of the Wash.

North-west of the Docking lies the long ridge of the Inner Dowsing. To the north-east of this, and running north-west to south-east, is the even longer Race Bank. Further to the north-east are the three shoals known as the Dudgeon, and beyond that the deep water Outer Dowsing Channel. The Admiralty Pilot for the area explains the problems faced by mariners: 'The shoals and sands are subject to constant changes . . . The tidal streams are long . . . the rise and fall of the tide considerable.'

The town of Skegness itself, at the southern end of the Lincolnshire coast, is perhaps best known as a holiday resort. Like most places in the area it has Viking origins: Skeggi's 'ness', or headland, was one of the places the Vikings landed in the ninth century. But the settlement was not particularly large with only a few hundred inhabitants, mostly working in fishing or farming, by the start of the nineteenth century. However, with the building of a railway during the 1870s, the town greatly expanded as visitors came in large numbers, most working class day-trippers from the East Midlands.

The Earl of Scarbrough was responsible for the initial development of the town during this period, employing an architect to create a 'watering place' on the site

Skegness lifeboats, lifeboat crew, station personnel and the local Coastguard outside the 1990-built lifeboat house in 2002. (By courtesy of RNLI Skegness)

of the existing village. The result was a new town with wide, tree-lined streets, promenades and gardens, a park and a pier, shopping streets, and new houses.

The new seaside town continued to grow, attracting more visitors each year. After the end of the First World War, Scarbrough sold to Skegness District Council, which continued the work and completed further amenities, including rose gardens, a boating lake and bathing pool, whilst new hotels and shops continued to spring up. Skegness suffered heavy bombing during the Second World War, and much repair work was undertaken during the late 1940s, together with improvements to the road system for the ever-increasing number of cars and lorries. Since the 1950s, caravan camps expanded on a huge scale to make Skegness the most popular caravan coast in the country.

The Skegness lifeboat station is an important part of this now thriving town, and has been for many years. Since the first lifeboat was stationed in the area, seafarers can be assured that, should they get into difficulty, rescuers are at hand. Since the lifeboat station was moved to the Promenade in 1990, becoming a prominent landmark on the beach front, the lifeboat has become an even greater focal point for both visitors and locals. The former come in their hundreds to look round the lifeboat house, admire the service boards listing the rescues, and see the gleaming boat on her carriage, with such visits almost as much a part of a holiday as candyfloss and sand castles.

Today, in 2008, the Skegness lifeboat is operated by a team of highly trained and dedicated volunteers, the latest in a long line willing to crew the boat and save lives at sea. Looking back, the crew has several notable family connections, as successive generations of Grunnill, Moody and Perrin family members have volunteered at various times. A Grunnill has been on the crew since the establishment of the station; the first motor mechanic was Percy Grunnill, while Mont Grunnill was Second Coxswain at the same time, and Joel Grunnill served as Second Coxswain and Honorary Secretary, and went on to become Chairman of the station.

Members of the Moody family have also been involved in the lifeboat, starting with Samuel Moody, famous Coxswain from 1830 for forty-one years. Joseph Moody and John Smith Moody both served as Coxswains during the later years of the nineteenth century. The Perrins have also given good service with George Perrin, a Gibraltar Point man, and Wilfred Perrin both serving as Coxswain during the early motor lifeboat era.

Acknowledgements

Many people have contributed to this history of the Skegness lifeboat station, but particular mention must go to Coxswain John Irving who was the driving force behind getting the project under way and whose support has been crucial to its success. The stories collected by the late Lt Cdr F. S. W. Major RNVR, and updated by former Coxswain Paul Martin, provided much useful detail, and I must acknowledge the debt I owe both. Grahame Farr's research into the operation of the Lincolnshire Coast Shipwreck Association also proved useful. Details of many of the rescues have come from published sources, mainly the RNLI's journal *The Lifeboat* and Annual Reports, and various local newspapers.

At the RNLI's headquarters in Poole, I am grateful to Barry Cox, the honorary librarian, and to Brian Wead and his staff in the Service Information Section for providing information, while Eleanor Driscoll and Nathan Williams supplied a number of photos for possible use. Jeff Morris kindly provided many excellent photos, which have considerably enhanced the book; photos by Ben Hardaker, Peter Edey and Gary Markham also proved useful. Others at the station gave information and photos, and of particular help has been Joel Grunnill, former Second Coxswain and Honorary Secretary; Graham Phillips, former Assistant Mechanic; and Ron Chapman, former Coxswain. Terry Despicht, current owner of *Anne Allen*, the only surviving Skegness lifeboat, kindly allowed me access to his boat. Finally, my gratitude as always to Sarah for her patience, support and help during my research and writing.

Nicholas Leach, May 2008

The first lifeboats

The first Skegness lifeboat, one of several operated along the Lincolnshire coast by a locally-run association, was quite successful in carrying out rescue work during the nineteenth century. At this time, trading vessels relied solely on sail for power, and the county's coast was as dangerous as any in the country. It offered no harbours of refuge, and, before Grimsby was developed as a port, had no harbour at all. Ships running from the weather had to make for either the Humber to the north, or the Wash to the south, and many were driven too close to shore to escape the expanse of shallow water and sandbanks which became a vast area of crashing surf during onshore gales. The area's earliest aid to the mariner was the Dudgeon lightvessel, established in 1734 and only the second floating light in United Kingdom waters. This warned ships away from the dangerous shore and was far enough offshore to make heading for either the Humber or the Wash a straightforward task.

Although shore-based lifeboats were built and operated elsewhere along the east coast between 1790 and 1820, none came to Lincolnshire. In 1812, Captain George William Manby, a Norfolk resident who was the inventor of the life-saving mortar for establishing communication between the shore and a wrecked ship, embarked on a tour of the east coast to examine provision for sea rescue and suggest improvements. Heading north from Yarmouth, he went as far as the Firth of Forth visiting towns, ports and harbours on his way. On completion of the tour, his *General Report on the Survey of the Eastern Coast of England* was published in 1813 which contained his findings. His information on Lincolnshire, which he visited during September 1812, included the following description:

'On commencing the survey of this county, I was struck with the extent of its shoals, and the consequent danger thereby presented; and the more so, when informed that numerous unseen shoals and over-falls laid off the coast, some newly created, some unnoticed in charts generally in use, and some having greatly increased, and extending themselves since a survey was taken.'

He advocated a floating light be established at Lynn Knock, but despite a public meeting held at Boston on 10 September 1812 at which it was resolved that this would be of great benefit, a Lynn Well lightvessel was not at its station until 1828. When he visited Skegness, Manby was told by Lieut Bunce, officer-in-charge of the signal station, that some strandings had been caused by the misinterpretation of lights at windows of the bathing houses and hotel. He wrote a letter to the Minister of the Parish Church calling on him to encourage parishioners to close their blinds at night. It is not known if this request was complied with, but Manby thought it unnecessary to send a mortar to Wainfleet or Skegness as he considered the floating light would give sufficient security for shipping.

Elsewhere in Lincolnshire, Manby described the shoals off Theddlethorpe and decided that 'as the people of this place are active and ready with their boats to give assistance, a six-pounder mortar should be sent.' He also provided his plan for converting boats as temporary lifeboats by means of casks lashed under the thwarts. When told of the dangers of Rose Shoals off Saltfleet and Hale Sand, which he noticed extended much further south than indicated on existing charts, he recommended a six-pounder mortar for use in a boat and for wrecks close inshore, and also a forty-two-pounder with much greater range for 'the relief of vessels when run upon the south end of the Hale sand.' Manby's recommendations were followed in part, and in January 1816, three twenty-four-pound brass mortars were sent to Saltfleet, Sutton and Skegness, where they were placed with the Waterguard, predecessors of the Coastguard.

However, despite the efforts and concerns of Manby, no lifeboats served the Lincolnshire coast until the middle of the 1820s, after the founding, on 4 March 1824, of the Royal National Institution for the Preservation of Life from Shipwreck (RNIPLS). The main motivator behind the new organisation, Sir William Hillary of Douglas in the Isle of Man, believed that a body, responsible for the preservation of life from shipwreck on a nationwide basis, was needed. The efforts of Sir William, together with Thomas Wilson and others, who met in London to set up the national body, involved looking at building, managing and funding lifeboats and the founding of new lifeboat stations, on a national basis.

The Institution established committees to consider the different aspects of life-saving work. One reviewed the types of lifeboat available, and another assessed the best places for stationing lifeboats and mortars. Captain William Bowles, RN, first Comptroller-General of the Coastguard, an organisation formed two years earlier, became involved in the latter committee, and sought the views of the Inspecting-

Commanders in the various Coastguard Districts. Port officials, such as Lloyd's Agents, harbourmasters, and pilot masters, also helped in these assessments, and the contribution of the Coastguard proved to be essential in assessing lifeboat needs between major ports and harbours.

In August 1824 Captain Wilson, RN, the Inspecting-Commander for Grimsby District, reported that a boat was needed three and a half miles south of Skegness at Gibraltar Point, also referred to as Boston Deeps or Wainfleet Haven, and a more secure and expansive haven than it is a century and more later. Seventy wrecks had occurred here in three years, with thirty men and three whole crews lost. In response to this request, when orders were placed for five lifeboats at a meeting of the Central Committee of the RNIPLS on 8 September 1824, one was allocated to the Point. The others went to Douglas, Plymouth, Courtmacsherry and Penzance.

The boats were ordered from William Plenty, a Newbury boatbuilder, whose design for a 24ft by 8ft craft rowing eight oars double-banked, steered by an oar, and manned by ten crew, was the Institution's first standard lifeboat design. A number of orders for Plenty's boats, regarded as particularly well suited for service in Lincolnshire, had been placed by the RNIPLS. The boats, with built-in air cases and a thick layer of cork on the bottom, were highly regarded and some had been used on Royal Navy ships employed in Arctic exploration.

The lifeboat for Gibraltar Point was not ready until September 1825, after Plenty had some difficulty finding sufficient workers at his yard, but once he received his payment of £130 for the boat, it was sent by sea and handed over to the Wainfleet Coastguard. Captain Wilson reported its arrival during October 1825, but also stated that neither a boathouse nor a local committee of management were in place, although William Skuffham was appointed Coxswain. Wilson was asked to help on a local level, and attempts were made to get funds for a house and organise a local committee.

However, the community in the vicinity of Gibraltar Point, made up largely of fishermen and pilots, was too small to undertake such matters. The nearest

Diagram of the Plenty lifeboat, the first type of rescue craft to be adopted as standard by the National Institution for the Preservation of Life from Shipwreck. The boats were between 18ft and 26ft in length, with the boat for Gibraltar Point 24ft long.

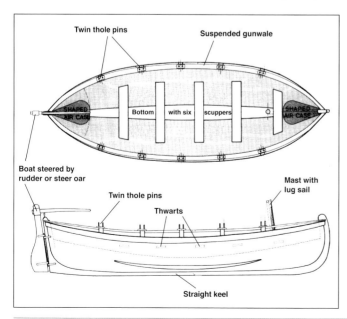

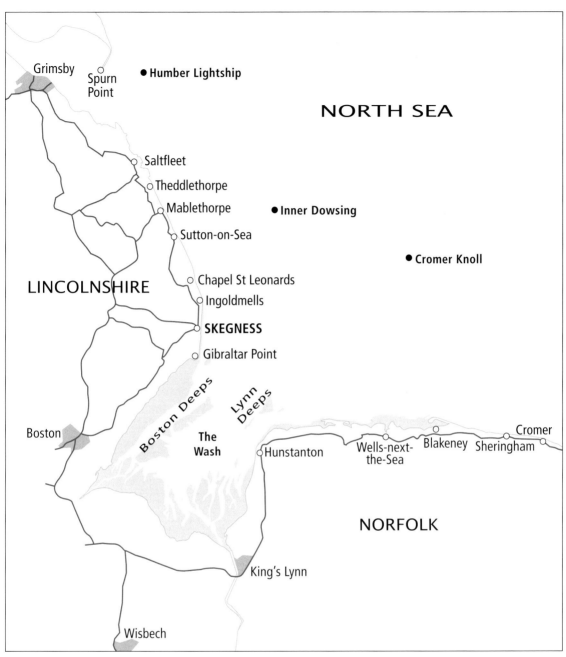

Grimsby
Spurn Point
● **Humber Lightship**

NORTH SEA

Saltfleet
Theddlethorpe
Mablethorpe
● **Inner Dowsing**
Sutton-on-Sea

● **Cromer Knoll**

LINCOLNSHIRE
Chapel St Leonards
Ingoldmells
SKEGNESS
Gibraltar Point

Boston Deeps
Lynn Deeps

Boston
The Wash
Hunstanton
Wells-next-the-Sea
Blakeney
Sheringham
Cromer

NORFOLK

King's Lynn

Wisbech

large town, Spilsby, was a more suitable place from which to raise awareness of the lifeboat and find the necessary funding and organisation for its operation. In October 1825, Charles Burrell Massingberd, of Ormsby Hall, Spilsby, became involved. He was Deputy Vice-Admiral of the County of Lincoln and, with his son Francis Charles Massingberd, Rector of Spilsby, devoted considerable time and effort to the Lincolnshire organisation in the next few years.

The Massingberds' interest may have been sparked by their witnessing a rescue off Ingoldmells. In a letter sent to the RNIPLS, Charles Massingberd describes the rescue on 28 October 1825 of the crew of the Finnish ship *Maria*, of Brahestad, using the mortar from Skegness, which was taken to Ingoldmells to effect the rescue. Lines were fired to the wreck, and using these two boats were hauled between wreck and land so that eleven men were saved. Two other men were drowned when

Map of the coasts of Lincolnshire and North Norfolk showing the major towns and sea marks. All of the coastal towns, apart from Ingoldmells, have or have had lifeboats.

they attempted to reach the shore in the ship's boat. Three Skegness men, Richard West, Samuel Moody and John Moody, were prominent among the rescuers, and were rewarded with £20 from London as well as donations received locally.

The letter which brought the £20 draft from London also reiterated the need for the formation of a local committee. Through the efforts of Charles Massingberd, with the support of the Vice-Admiral of the county, Earl Brownlow, such a body was established at a meeting at Spilsby Town Hall on 23 January 1826. It was formally launched as the Spilsby District Committee 'in Union with the Royal National Institution'. Its role was to manage the Gibraltar Point lifeboat and the mortar apparatus at Skegness. This new body was one of a number of county and regional lifeboat societies that were established during the first half of the nineteenth century, operating independently but affiliated to the RNIPLS. When Sir William Hillary founded the national institution, he envisaged local committees and associations acting under the broad

general directions of the RNIPLS' central committee with regard to lifeboat types, standards of crewing and remuneration, and in receiving grants collected from a wider national catchment area, and the Spilsby Committee was such a body.

Three months after its establishment, the Spilsby Committee considered ideas for expanding the life-saving service in the county, and began to consider what might be needed elsewhere along the county's coasts. They decided that a boat was needed near the Humber, and also wanted a mortar at Mumby Chapel. The Skegness mortar had been left at Ingoldmells after the successful *Maria* rescue, and the Coastguard queried the idea of placing another only about a mile further along. However, the application was approved and both a twenty-four-pounder brass and a six-pounder iron mortar were sent to Mumby Chapel in August 1826.

A campaign by the Vice-Admiral and his Deputy followed, and this raised support from the whole county. A year and a half after the foundation of the Spilsby District Committee, support was deemed to be sufficiently broad based to promote a

Painting of the first Skegness lifeboat, the Plenty-built boat, going to the rescue of the brig Hermione in 1833 with Coxswain Samuel Moody at her helm. This painting hangs in the present lifeboat house.

County Association along the same lines as those which had been in existence for several years in Essex, Norfolk and Suffolk. The formal announcement read:

> 'At a Meeting of the Nobility, Justices, Grand Jurors, and Gentry, held in the Grand Jury Room, at the Castle of Lincoln, on Tuesday, the 31st day of July, 1827, in pursuance of a requisition to the Lord Lieutenant and Vice-Admiral of the County; the Right Hon the Earl Brownlow, in the Chair. It was resolved unanimously that it is expedient to form a County Association for the protection of lives and property from shipwreck on the coast of Lincolnshire, in union with the Royal National Institution for the same purpose.'

Earl Brownlow consented to act as Patron, Lord Yarborough as President, and a number of others including the Duke of St Albans, Lord Willoughby de Broke, and Lord Gwydir, together with C. B. Massingberd and the Mayors of Lincoln, Boston and Grimsby, and the Warden of Louth, were requested to act as Vice-Presidents. The posts of secretary and treasurer were filled by William Forbes, of Sleaford, and Joseph Brackenbury, of Spilsby, respectively.

The chosen title was the Lincolnshire Coast Association, but three years later the word Shipwreck was added. At the same time a central management committee was established under C. B. Massingberd with Rev F. C. Massingberd as secretary, acting as a link between the various district committees which were set up as the work expanded along the coast.

By the time the new Association had come into existence, the sole lifeboat in the county, that at Gibraltar Point, had performed its first service. On 21 January 1827 she launched to a vessel, apparently drifting out of control, and found the ship *Stirling*, of South Shields, abandoned by her crew. The lifeboatmen boarded the ship and brought her to a safe anchorage. For the salvage of ship and cargo, Massingberd secured the sum of £146 10s 0d which was divided amongst the rescuers.

In 1827, the LCSA established its second station, at Saltfleet, with a second-hand lifeboat purchased from Bridlington in Yorkshire, built by Henry Greathead, of South Shields, in 1805. However, it was

disliked by the Saltfleet boatmen who had to operate it, and proved too large for the limited crew available there. As a result, in 1829 it was moved to Donna Nook, where a tragedy during the preceding winter had seen the loss of three seamen. As the Greathead boat had proven not to be totally suitable, the LCSA, at its first Annual Meeting on 29 July 1828, ordered another lifeboat from Plenty, intended for Donna Nook. Although ordered in August 1828, this boat was not ready until 1829, by when the Greathead boat had been transferred to Donna Nook. When the Plenty boat eventually reached Lincolnshire, it was placed at Theddlethorpe.

By this time, discussions had taken place with regard to moving the Gibraltar Point lifeboat to Skegness. The LCSA committee hesitated initially because the RNIPLS had chosen the station on the advice of experienced Coastguards as a place where the boat could be got afloat in all weathers. However, a wreck on Skegness Middle bank on 20 January 1830 suggested that the boat should be moved, while part of the Manby apparatus had already been moved to Skegness for the crew to use when pulling the lifeboat from the shore.

The incident in January 1830 which resulted in the lifeboat's transfer involved the sloop *Thomas and Mary*, of Wells, which went aground at about 10am and sank, forcing the four crew into the rigging. The vessel was out of range of a mortar, so a messenger was sent to summon the lifeboat, four miles south. A faulty wheel on the truck delayed the lifeboat's immediate despatch, so John Bell, a Skegness fisherman, went out in his own boat and, at considerable risk, took off one man. Another man had lost his grip in the rigging and drowned. As the storm

The Palmer type lifeboat as depicted in a line drawing from the Select Committee on Shipwrecks of 1843. It shows the 1828 version of the design, which was 26ft 8in in length and 6ft 2in in beam.

worsened, further attempts by ordinary boats were impossible but, with the tide receding, a mortar line was got across to the wreck. By this time, however, the two survivors were so numb that they could not secure the line.

Soon afterwards, the lifeboat arrived and it was immediately launched into the heavy surf. Captain Wyborn, RN, the Inspecting Officer of the Coastguard, witnessed the events and later said he had considered, because of the violence of the storm, trying to dissuade them from the rescue attempt. However, the lifeboat crew was determined and eventually returned with the two survivors, practically frozen after their six-hour ordeal in the rigging. John Bell and his crew were rewarded, as was the lifeboat crew under William Skuffham, with John Grunnill praised for 'conspicuous exertions' having boarded the wreck to free the two survivors from the rigging.

Soon after this incident, the boat was moved permanently to Skegness because, in northerly and north-easterly gales, at Gibraltar Point it was found to be too far to leeward of the sandbanks on which vessels, running to shelter in the Wash, were likely to founder. A site for a boathouse at Skegness was obtained among the dunes, at the back of what later became known as Lifeboat Avenue. The Gibraltar Point house was then dismantled and moved north at a cost of £28, with an extra £9 16s 0d for a new launching truck. A further £9 10s 0d was provided to pay for the addition to the house of a 'sleeping room' for the master, or Coxswain, who was then Samuel Moody. Moody followed William Skuffham as Coxswain in 1830 and served for forty-one years, becoming one of the station's most notable nineteenth century lifeboatmen.

In 1829 the practical work of the Association was divided into three districts, each having its own local committee. These consisted of Spilsby, managing the lifeboat at Gibraltar Point (soon moved to Skegness), and Manby's apparatus at Skegness; Louth, with a lifeboat at Theddlethorpe, and apparatus at Ingoldmells and Theddlethorpe; and the Northern District, with a lifeboat at Donna Nook, which had just been moved from Saltfleet, and apparatus at Saltfleet.

The following year, the Gibraltar Point boat was moved, described above, and the Greathead boat at Donna Nook was broken up after being condemned as beyond economical repair. In 1831 the Theddlethorpe boat was transferred to Donna Nook.

In August, the Rev Massingberd wrote to the Institution asking about the Palmer design, another type of lifeboat then being developed. The Institution lent the LCSA a ship's boat which had been altered to the Palmer plan, and, as it was found to be suitable, the local body resolved to obtain a boat of the type. The Palmer type boat that was ordered, from Bell & Grange, a boatbuilder of Grimsby, was 25ft 9in in length and was delivered to Donna Nook in 1832, enabling the Plenty boat to be returned to Theddlethorpe.

The next lifeboat north of Skegness was at Huttoft, or Huttoft Bank, another Bell & Grange-built craft, completed in 1835 and 22ft 6in in length. The Huttoft station was established following an unfortunate failure, on 24 October 1834, of the mortar apparatus brought from Sutton to aid the brig *Betty*, of Lynn, which had been driven ashore in heavy weather, although the mortar was not the responsibility of the LCSA. In 1844, the Huttoft boat was moved to Sutton when it was also suggested that a small boat should be stationed at Ingoldmells, although details of a boat, if one was sent, are lacking.

Of the various lifeboats operated by the LCSA, by far the most successful was the 1825-built Plenty boat, at Skegness from 1830, which is credited with at least sixteen services and the saving of sixty-three lives and five vessels during almost four decades on station. One of her first services from Skegness took place during a terrible storm on 31 August and 1 September 1833 during which at least seven ships stranded with most becoming wrecks. The brig *Hermione*, of London, went ashore at Skegness about noon on 31 August and her boat was swamped as it was put into the water. The brig was out of range of the mortar, so the lifeboat was launched and, after a struggle for her crew to pull through the heavy seas, brought ashore all ten of her crew.

Early the next day, the brig *Agenoria*, of Plymouth, was driven ashore at

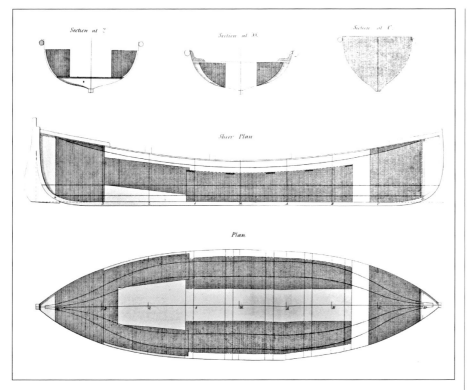

Ingoldmells. It was almost too dark to see the wreck, but under the superintendence of John Booth, the mortar was prepared and fired. A break in the clouds twenty minutes later, with the moon lighting the scene, showed the line lying between the masts of the brig and the crew making it fast. A boat was soon hauled out to the wreck and brought all nine survivors safely to shore. Booth was later presented with an inscribed silver plate in recognition of his leadership during this rescue.

On 24 January 1838, the lifeboat completed an outstanding rescue when she went to the sloop *Boyne*, of Goole, which was wrecked between Skegness and Ingoldmells. After a great struggle, the lifeboat crew reached the casualty but had rescued just one man when a huge sea broke the lines holding the rescuers to the wreck. The boat was driven back to the shore in some disorder, but no sooner had the crew scrambled out when two crew members, Grunnill and Moody, rushed back into the surf and grabbed a rope sent ashore from the sloop, by which means they pulled another man to safety. A boy had already died from exposure. The two quick-thinking men were awarded medals by the Association.

On 28 August 1838, the LCSA's annual meeting and display of lifeboats was held at Mablethorpe, and on returning to their station the Skegness crew found the sloop *Foggy*, of Sunderland, had drifted ashore in calm weather on the Outer Knock Sand. Her crew refused help, but during the night the wind increased and the lifeboat again went out to her. Unfortunately, the tide was too low for them to cross the bank straight to the casualty and a detour had to be made round its south side, with the sea getting increasingly heavy. When the lifeboat was almost alongside, a huge sea capsized the wreck and also struck the lifeboat, putting her on her beam ends. Four oars were lost overboard, along with one of the crew, but he was recovered immediately by the other crew members. However, the three men on board *Foggy* were drowned before anything could be done to help them.

Less than a year later, the lifeboat completed another successful rescue when, on 9 April 1839, she saved the crew of four from the skiff *Anna Margueretta*, of Hamburg. Laden with rape cake, the skiff sank at high water after going aground, and her crew of four refused to leave even when warned of the danger they

Samuel Moody, Coxswain from 1830 to 1871, was one of the station's most notable nineteenth century lifeboatmen. (By courtesy of Skegness RNLI)

were in. At first two local men, Richard Houghton and Thomas Green, tried to take them off in their coble, but the attempt was unsuccessful and the rescuers were swept back to shore. The lifeboat was then launched and reached the skiff after a long struggle for the crew. It took the survivors on board and landed them safely. A month later the lifeboat went to the sloop *Free Briton*, which had broken her anchor during a gale. The lifeboat crew found the sloop deserted, the crew having landed on the Norfolk coast in their own boat, but stood by until the casualty became a wreck.

Detailed information about rescues undertaken during the 1840s is lacking, although brief accounts were included in the LCSA's annual statements. In November 1841, the Skegness boat saved three from the Wisbech vessel *Jane*, and on 27 February 1844, fifteen were saved from the steam packet *City of Carlisle*, of Liverpool. On 3 May 1846 the lifeboat went to the Inner Knock Sand and saved the *Speed*, of Boston, and on 13 October 1848, the Skegness crew saved the galliot *Anna Maria*, bound from Bremen for Hull, from the Dogshead Sand, although exact numbers of men saved from these vessels is not specified.

During the 1840s and 1850s, the LCSA and its lifeboats continued operating with some success, but on a national level the RNIPLS was not faring so well. Financial problems led to only a handful of new lifeboats being built, with problems maintaining those already in existence. With no public appeals made for almost a decade, by 1850 the national body's income was at its lowest level. However, reforms to enable the Institution to continue its work took place during the 1850s after the fourth Duke of Northumberland, then First Lord of the Admiralty, became President.

Before becoming President, in May 1850 the Duke organised a national competition to test the ideas of the nation's boatbuilders and designers and find an improved design of lifeboat. The plans, of which 282 were submitted, were published in an official Report in 1851 which also listed the lifeboat stations then in existence, and included a brief description of life-saving facilities at each. The boats at Donna Nook, Theddlethorpe, Sutton and Skegness all merited an entry, with the latter two boats described as being 'in fair repair; pulls fairly'.

A copy of the Northumberland Report was sent to the LCSA in 1851 with the compliments of the Duke, but it contained a small item that apparently offended the officers of the Association. The Report referred to the Gibraltar Point lifeboat as being 'placed and supported' by the National Shipwreck Institution. That it was placed by them in the care of a local body, the Spilsby District Association, was not disputed. However, the successors to the original body, the LCSA, had assumed responsibility for its housing, repairs and support. The view of the RNIPLS was that, having given the boat in the first place but received no support, the boat was still under their auspices.

To rectify matters, the LCSA voluntarily gave £50 'in gratitude for the bestowal of the boat in the first place' and the matter was quickly resolved. The Institution furthered positive relations by awarding Coxswain Samuel Moody the Silver medal in recognition of his 'gallant and persevering conduct, in having been instrumental, under divine Providence, in saving so many lives from shipwreck'. He had, by this time, assisted in saving fifty-three lives, including some rescues effected in his own boat.

On 27 December 1852 Moody and his men were prominent in two rescues. The first was undertaken using his own boat, in which he went out with four lifeboatmen to the sloop *Lee*, of Lynn, bound for Lynn with coal from Goole. She had already sunk and lost her own boat by the time Moody was afloat, but from her rigging three men were saved. Later, the schooner *William*, also of Lynn, and homeward bound with coal, got into difficulty. She was driven ashore at Skegness having lost her anchor, her sails and her boat, and the lifeboat saved her crew of five.

A fine service took place on 18 October 1854 when the brig *Atalanta*, of Shields, carrying a cargo of timber which was on fire, went ashore at about 6pm three miles north of Skegness in a north-easterly gale. The lifeboat on its carriage was drawn by six horses to the scene, where it was prepared for launching. It was extremely dark, and huge waves were breaking on the shore when the lifeboat put out, but she succeeded in bringing ashore nine men and the master's wife and child from the brig. *Atalanta* continued burning on the beach until the following morning. On the same night, twenty-two vessels were driven ashore between Skegness and the mouth of the Humber, and the Sutton lifeboat was also in action. For this rescue, Coxswain Samuel Moody was awarded a second service clasp to his Silver medal.

The last services of Skegness' first lifeboat were both undertaken in February 1860. On 17 February she saved three from the sloop *Alert*, of Grimsby, on the Dogshead Sand, which was badly damaged and without a rudder. The lifeboat crew reached the casualty just in time to find the crew about to abandon ship in a small leaky boat. So they were taken on board the lifeboat, and the sloop was towed to Boston. On 28 February the lifeboat went out to the sloop *Joseph and Ann*, of Gainsborough, which was aground on the Inner Knock Sand and flying distress signals. However, the gale abated before the lifeboat's services were required. The sloop's crew decided not to leave, although the lifeboat stood by until the vessel was safe.

The RNLI takes over

By the time of this service, the future of Lincolnshire's lifeboat stations had become uncertain. In 1863 the LCSA, the last of the County Associations which was still operating independently of the RNLI, realised that its stations needed completely renovating. Its four lifeboats were old and worn out, three of the transporting carriages required replacing, and the boathouses were too small to accommodate larger boats and their necessary equipment. The cost of providing the necessary replacements would have forced the LCSA to use almost all of their invested capital of £1,700.

The old boathouse at Donna Nook, pictured after the station had closed but before the hosue was demolished. The Donna Nook station was established in 1829 and closed in 1931. During 102 years of service, its lifeboats launched eighty-six times on service and saved 172 lives. The last three lifeboats, from 1879, were all named Richard, and were provided by Miss Dixon, of Caistor, in North Lincolnshire. (By courtesy of Grahame Farr)

The lifeboat house moved to Skegness from Gibraltar Point in 1830 and used until 1864. This boathouse was situated in Lifeboat Avenue and was reached by a wide pathway. The horses which pulled the lifeboat to and from the water were brought from the Vine Hotel. The lookout tower on the right was erected in the sand dunes at the same time that the house was moved north. (By courtesy of Skegness RNLI)

The Association realised that continuing independently would therefore be very difficult and so the central committee decided that amalgamation with the RNLI was the only way forward.

At the biennial inspection and exhibition of the lifeboats, which took place at Mablethorpe on 30 July 1863, the Honorary Secretary, the Rev J. Arlington, approached the RNLI's District Inspector, Captain John R. Ward, RN, about some form of union with the national body. During the public dinner which took place afterwards, Captain Ward took the opportunity of explaining how advantageous this would be, and, in

January 1864, the matter was resolved. The LCSA governing body met at Spilsby on 11 January with Captain Ward also in attendance. He explained that cooperation was offered primarily to improve the efficiency of the lifeboat establishments, rather than because of the extra revenue contributed by the Association. The main condition of union was that the LCSA would provide £600 in funds, and the four stations on the Lincolnshire coast would be completely renovated by the RNLI. In addition, the crews would receive quarterly training, something that local funds had not hitherto permitted.

By the end of 1864 the Institution had fulfilled its principal obligation. Four new lifeboats and four new carriages had been provided for the county's four lifeboat stations, and four new boathouses had been built, with a total expenditure of £2,054 15s 9d. During the thirty-nine years that the LCSA lifeboat was stationed at Skegness, seventy-six lives were saved, either by the lifeboat itself or by its crew in their own boats. During this time, the longshoremen of Lincolnshire frequently showed their skill and bravery in helping seamen in trouble using lifeboats and mortars, on horseback, or by just dashing into the surf, the last two methods being possible because of the peculiarly flat shores, typical of the county's beaches.

The old lifeboat house at Chapel St Leonards, eight miles north of Skegness, where the RNLI stationed three lifeboats from 1870 until 1898, credited with saving fourteen lives. (Nicholas Leach)

Herbert Ingram lifeboats

When it took over the running of Skegness lifeboat station in the 1860s, the RNLI was enjoying a period of expansion with its healthy financial situation enabling it to establish many new stations. As soon as the LCSA's four stations had been taken over, all were completely renovated as the boats and carriages used by the Association were worn out. New lifeboats, each 30ft long and 7ft 3in wide, were supplied. All built by Forrestt, the Institution's boatbuilder at Limehouse, the boats had eight oars double-banked to suit the local boatmen used to rowing with double-banked short oars.

They were built to the RNLI's self-righting design, which had been developed during the 1850s and saw widespread use throughout the late nineteenth century around the coasts of the British Isles and Ireland. Transporting carriages were also supplied to each station, and 'commodious and substantial lifeboat houses' erected. All the boats and carriages were conveyed to their destinations free of charge by the Great Northern Railway Company.

The new lifeboats and carriages were funded by different donors at each station. For Donna Nook, £350 was presented to the Institution by Robert How, of London, and Miss How, his sister, and the new lifeboat was named *North Briton* after a ship in which the donors had enjoyed a long voyage. The same amount was needed at Theddlethorpe, where the gift of Mrs Barbara Caslake and her friend was used to provide a lifeboat named *Dorinda and Barbara*. The cost of the Sutton lifeboat was collected in Birmingham, mainly through the exertions of Alderman Holliday, Henry Fulford, and others, and the boat was named *Birmingham*. Before being sent to its station, this lifeboat was taken to Birmingham where it was publicly exhibited on 29 November 1864 in the city centre.

The new Skegness boat was funded by the family and friends of Herbert Ingram, MP for Boston, who had been drowned with his son when the steamer *Lady Elgin* was lost with 287 persons in a disaster on Lake Michigan in America in 1860. Ingram, born in May 1811 and probably Boston's most famous person, was apprenticed to local printer Joseph Clarke after his education. He then moved to London where, in 1842, he founded the *Illustrated London News*. Newspapers of the time were wordy, text-only affairs, so when he introduced illustrations to go with the stories he was ahead of his time and sales soared. From March 1856 he was MP for Boston and played a major part in getting a fresh water supply piped to the town as well as being instrumental in bringing the railway to the town.

The new lifeboat named in his honour arrived by rail at his home town on 24 October 1864. After being paraded through the streets, she was christened *Herbert Ingram* by Mrs J. H. Thomas at a ceremony held in the Market Place, at which a 'large assemblage of persons' were present. The ceremony and naming took

Line drawing showing the deck plan and sheer plan of the RNLI's self-righting lifeboats of the 1860s and 1870s. Although this was a generic drawing used throughout the RNLI's publications of the time, it shows a boat similar in appearance to the first Herbert Ingram.

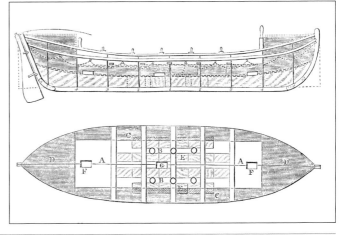

The four lifeboat stations taken over by the RNLI were, in addition to Skegness, those at Theddlethorpe, Sutton and Donna Nook. The station at Sutton was established by the LCSA in 1844 and this lifeboat house was built there in 1864 when the Institution took over operations; it was used until the station closed in 1913. Still standing and largely unaltered, it is situated between the sea wall and the main road, and was converted into the Merridale Hall for use by the Merridale Youth and Community Centre. The lifeboat house built at Skegness in 1864 would have been similar in appearance to this. (Nicholas Leach)

Line drawing showing the RNLI's standard launching carriage used with self-righting lifeboats during the 1860s and 1870s. This is the kind of carriage that would have been used at Skegness at this time.

place in front of a monument to Ingram, in the presence of the mayor, members of the town council, and other principal inhabitants of the town. In preparation for the boat, a new lifeboat house was built, at a cost of £180, half a mile south of the main pullover. Part of the house remained standing into the 1980s as a private dwelling in the area of Lifeboat and Marine Avenues.

The first launch of the new lifeboat was to the ketch *Grouse*, of Wells, on the afternoon of 20 February 1865. The ketch was carrying coals from Hartlepool to Wells with three crew on board, including the master, when she went ashore at the tail of Wainfleet Sand, near Gibraltar Point. She had parted her anchors in the

Humber, her sails had split and she was leaking. Forty minutes after launching in a strong northerly gale with squally snow showers, *Herbert Ingram* reached the stranded vessel, but the master refused to leave and the lifeboat returned to her station without completing her service.

Herbert Ingram was called out twice on 2 December 1867. She first went to the 210-ton brig *Claudia*, of Sunderland, which had run aground at low water at Ingoldmells Point. A violent northerly wind was blowing, and the lifeboat on her carriage, pulled by five horses, was taken the three miles to Ingoldmells along the beach, a faster and easier journey than rowing through the heavy seas. On reaching Ingoldmells, the lifeboatmen found that the Sutton lifeboat was already on scene and had taken off the crew of seven, so their services were not required.

However, whilst at Ingoldmells, the lifeboat crew saw signals of distress flying from the sloop *Ant*, of Boston, which was on her way to Goole. So *Herbert Ingram* launched into the strong gale and, after an hour pulling through snow showers, reached the casualty at 5pm. The vessel had parted both anchor cables off the Bull lightship, and her two crew were completely exhausted. They were quickly taken off by the lifeboat, which beached at Skegness at 7pm, and *Ant* subsequently became a total wreck.

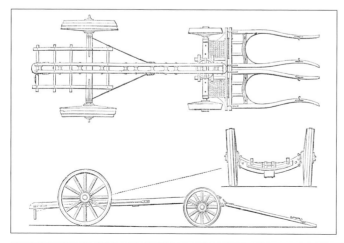

Three collier brigs went aground on the Knock sands during a strong north-easterly gale on 30 September 1871. The first, the 200-ton *Regina* of London, with a crew of seven, was seen by the Coxswain, Thomas Green, showing signals of distress and the lifeboat was immediately launched. She soon reached the vessel and succeeded in bringing its crew ashore. Almost as soon as the lifeboat had landed, she was launched again and made for the other two vessels, which were reached after a hard struggle for the crew.

As they took the seven crew off *Orb*, of Whitby, heavy seas broke over the lifeboat, her crew and the survivors. Despite this, they made for the third vessel, the 182-ton *James*, of Dover, whose crew of eight refused to leave and so the lifeboat headed for shore. Shortly afterwards the crew of *James* had to leave in their own boat as the brig became a total wreck. The rescue took place in the space of an hour, the lifeboat launching at 11am, reaching the casualties half an hour later, and returning to the beach at 12 noon.

On 10 November 1873, the lifeboat launched in an easterly gale to assist two vessels, the barque *Francoise Marie*, of Caen, and the brig *Die Schwalbe*, of Rostock, in distress off Skegness. Seven men were saved from the barque, ten from the brig, and the lifeboat helped to salvage both vessels. However, following this service, the wrecks became part of a property salvage case and matters took a turn for the worse. Five days after the service, the Inspector, Captain J. H. Ward, visited the station and found Coxswain Thomas Green half drunk while the lifeboat carriage, according to his report, was 'in a dirty and neglected state, the ventilating hatches being on, and some of the gear out of the boat'. Ward was told that, since the service on 10 November, Green had not been sober, while 'other irregularities had also taken place in connection with the employment of the boat in saving the two foreign vessels'.

Ward attended a meeting of the local committee on 19 November, with the Rev E. Morson in the chair, to determine what course of action should be taken in light of the findings. At the meeting it was stated that Coxswain Green's two sons had made salvage arrangements after the service nine days earlier, and received and shared the money without consulting either the Coxswain or the Honorary Secretary.

The minutes of the meeting stated that they 'appeared to have taken control of the boat out of the Coxswain's hands and . . . also behaved in a very unbecoming and insolent manner at the meeting; wanted to know when they would be paid for their services . . . and on the

An early print of the first Herbert Ingram lifeboat on her launching carriage. She was typical of the RNLI's early self-righting type, and served the station for ten years.

Inspector informing them they were not likely to be paid for services which they received salvage payments, they became very abusive'. As Green was 'shown to be addicted to drinking to excess and had no command over his crew', the committee had little choice but to suspend him, appointing Second Coxswain Thomas Moody in his place.

At the same meeting of the committee, the crew complained that the lifeboat was cramped and so the Inspector recommended that another lifeboat be sent to the station. On 4 December 1873 arrangements were made for the former Thorpeness lifeboat to be supplied, together with a carriage, transferred from Southport. Meanwhile, on 19 March 1874, the first *Herbert Ingram* performed what proved to be her last service when she stood by the sloop *New Eagle*, of Grimsby, which was in difficulty off Ingoldmells in south-westerly winds.

The station's next lifeboat reached Skegness on 9 April 1874 having been carried free of charge on the Great Northern Railway. This lifeboat, built by Forrestt at Limehouse in 1866, had been stationed at Gorleston from 1866 to 1870 during which time she was named *Leicester*, and was then at Thorpeness from 1870 to 1873 named *Ipswich*. When transferred to Skegness, she was appropriated to the gift of the family and friends of Herbert Ingram, after whom she was named. At 33ft in length, the second *Herbert Ingram* was 'larger and more commodious' than the boat she replaced, according to *The Lifeboat* of 1 August 1874. She pulled ten oars, as opposed to eight on her predecessor, and was manned by a crew of thirteen. During her fourteen years at Skegness, this lifeboat launched twenty-three times on service and is credited with saving twenty-seven lives.

Less than three weeks after *Herbert Ingram* arrived, tragedy struck after an exercise launch on 28 April 1874. The lifeboat had been at sea for about an hour and had sailed close to the shore, impressing the crew with her capabilities. She was then recovered but, while being dragged across the beach to the lifeboat house, the carriage sank into the wet sand. The horses were unable to pull it free, so seventeen-year-old Matthew Hildred went with an additional horse to offer further help. The launchers then succeeded in moving the boat but, when leading the horse, Hildred was knocked down onto the sands and before he could get out of the way, the wheel of the carriage ran him over, killing him immediately.

The first service by the second *Herbert Ingram* took place on 5 December 1875 after the sixty-three-ton ketch-rigged barge *Star*, of Colchester, bound from Hull to Poole, with a cargo of timber and three crew, was driven ashore at Winthorpe Gap at 4.30am. The weather was bitterly cold, and the fresh easterly gale was accompanied by heavy snow showers. On her carriage pulled by horses, *Herbert Ingram* was taken two miles along the beach to be launched through the considerable surf at 6am. Getting afloat was difficult because of the strong winds blowing across the exposed beach but, twenty minutes later, the lifeboat reached the stranded vessel. It was surrounded by broken water a few hundred yards out,

A posed photograph of Joseph Grunnill, a crew member for forty-two years from 1867 to 1909 and bowman from 1900 to 1909. He retired on 25 November 1909 aged sixty-three, and was presented with a framed copy of this picture, together with a clock, by Admiral Buckle RN, chairman of the station committee. (By courtesy of Skegness RNLI)

and the lifeboatmen had some difficulty getting the crew off.

Two were safely got aboard the lifeboat, but the master, the last to leave, fell overboard and, without a lifebelt, was in danger of being swept away. Immediately, two lifeboatmen, George Chesnutt and Samuel Moody (namesake of the former Coxswain), jumped in to help and, wearing their lifebelts, were able to support the master and bring him alongside the lifeboat. As it was impossible to get them back on board the boat, they held on to the boat's lines as it was pulled ashore. Fortunately the lifeboat was only a few hundred yards off the beach. Both Chesnutt and Moody were awarded Silver medals by the RNLI for their selfless actions during this service.

The next service proved to be another difficult one. At 8.30am on 14 April 1876, the ketch *Elizabeth*, of Goole, en route from London to Gainsborough, was seen in distress off Skegness, after colliding with another vessel in an onshore gale with snow showers. The vessel was watched by those on the shore as she swamped on striking the sandbanks. Her masts remained above the water and her crew lashed themselves in the rigging. *Herbert Ingram* was readied for launching, but the

first two attempts to get her away failed and she was washed back onto the beach, broadside on, by the heavy surf.

At about 9.30am, at the third attempt, she got clear of the beach, and half an hour later was alongside the casualty. Two men were saved from the rigging, but a third man died before the lifeboat could get to him, although a fourth man, thought to have been lost overboard, was picked up by the brigantine which had collided with *Elizabeth*.

The rescue in which *Herbert Ingram* saved the most lives took place on 23 March 1881, and it proved to be a particularly testing one for the crew. Distress signals were seen from a vessel ashore on the Knock Sands and so the lifeboat launched immediately into a south-south-easterly gale and heavy seas. The conditions proved too difficult, the lifeboat filled three times, two of her oars were broken, and she was driven ashore two miles south of her station. But the lifeboatmen and shore crew persevered, and recovered her onto her carriage for another launch. Three extra crew were taken to double-man the oars, and this time she succeeded in reaching the vessel, which was the barque *Lom*, of Hudiksval, Sweden, bound to Bilbao with a cargo of

The last Chapel St Leonards lifeboat, John Alexander Berrey, which was on station from 1888 to 1898. When this boat was withdrawn the station, situated to the north of Skegness, was closed. The boat's Coxswain was Matthew Grunnill, who later moved to the Skegness crew. He was part of a seafaring family which had long vied with the Moodys for the honour of putting the most men in the Skegness boat. He was also the son of the first Coxswain of the Chapel lifeboat, Edward Grunnill. (By courtesy of Joel Grunnill)

A posed photograph of Thomas Smalley, Coxswain from 1880 to 1900, who first joined the crew in 1873. He had to retire through ill health, and died on 16 November 1903, aged fifty-four. (By courtesy of Skegness RNLI)

deals and boards. The barque's ten crew were taken off and brought ashore by the lifeboat, which was then recovered.

During 1883, *Herbert Ingram* completed two effective services. The first was to the sloop *Good Intent*, of King's Lynn, on 30 September 1883. The sloop had lost her main boom and her sails had been blown away while she was bound to her home port from Seaham with coal. She was seen about five miles east of Skegness and so, at the master's request, the lifeboat escorted her to Lynn Roads. The second service was on 12 December 1883 to the

steamship *Victoria*, of Goole, which got into difficulty in a north-westerly gale. The lifeboat put off and, when to windward of the casualty, dropped anchor. She then bore down on the vessel and, after several attempts, got a line aboard after which the master and three crew were taken on board. The steamer was leaking and sank just as the lifeboat was landing its crew at Brancaster, in Norfolk.

The final services performed by *Herbert Ingram* took place at the beginning and end of 1888. The first was on 28 January to the thirty-two-ton brig *Starbeam*, of and for Boston, which got into difficulty in rough seas and a strong northerly breeze. She was carrying a cargo of ice when she stranded on the Dogshead Sandbank and started leaking. However, with the help of the lifeboat crew, she was refloated at 3pm and escorted by the lifeboat to Boston.

The second service took place on 21 November and was a long drawn-out affair. *Herbert Ingram* launched at 8.45am to the sloop *New Superior*, of Boston, which was in difficulty. The lifeboat crew reached the casualty to find that its mainsail had been blown away. The master asked the lifeboatmen to take a telegram ashore which was requesting a new mainsail be sent to Boston by the next train, so the vessel could be re-rigged using this new sail on her arrival in port. At 3.45pm a pilot cutter attempted to take the vessel in tow, but the hawser broke. The lifeboat then put out to her again, taking a yawl sail as a temporary measure, and escorting the vessel to a safe mooring.

Donna Nook's last lifeboat, a 34ft Rubie self-righting type named Richard, which served from 1904 to 1921, being hauled across the beach by an early lifeboat launching tractor. The carriage has Tipping's plates fitted to stop the wheels sinking into the sand.

The last pulling lifeboats

The matter of supplying a new lifeboat to Skegness had arisen in June 1887 when the Chief Inspector visited the station to assess the condition of *Herbert Ingram*, and he questioned whether she retained her self-righting capability. As this was in doubt, in June 1888 the RNLI's Committee of Management decided that a new lifeboat should be built for the station. So an order was placed at the yard of D. & W. Henderson & Co, of Glasgow, for a 37ft self-righter, pulled by twelve oars and manned by a crew of fifteen.

She was fitted with water ballast tanks, standing lug and jib sails with a no.1 rig and steel tabernacle mizen. The new lifeboat passed her harbour trial at Glasgow on 6 October 1888 and on 13 December 1888 a legacy of £500, bequeathed to the RNLI by the late Miss Ann Ball, of Balls Pond, London, was appropriated to the new lifeboat. The terms of the legacy stated that the money should fund a lifeboat for the Lincolnshire coast to be named *Ann, John and Mary*.

On 28 December 1888 the new lifeboat left Glasgow by rail and the following day arrived at Skegness where she was unloaded and taken to her new station. A carriage, previously at the Hauxley station in Northumberland, was sent and the old carriage was sold locally, as was the old lifeboat *Herbert Ingram*. *Ann, John and Mary* had the traditional lug-sail yawl rig of the Lincolnshire and Norfolk coasts. She served the station for almost twenty years, and is credited with saving thirteen lives. She was taken to sea in rough weather for the first time in May 1889, and the crew expressed their surprise at how much better she handled the poor conditions than the old boat.

With the arrival of the new lifeboat, the launching arrangements were reviewed. Problems with launching off the open beach had regularly been encountered, and dragging the carriage across the soft sand could be difficult. At the time, the RNLI was looking at building slipways with boathouses at their head, which not only speeded up launching but was also a

Ann, John and Mary being hauled across the beach on her carriage by a team of horses, with the pier in the background. (From an old postcard in the author's collection)

far easier way to get the boat afloat than from a carriage, which required horses and a large number of shore helpers.

In May 1890 the 1864-built boathouse was enlarged as it was too small for the new lifeboat, but even then the building was still somewhat inadequate, and so alternatives were examined. In June 1890 the District Inspector proposed that, rather than adapting and improving the existing lifeboat house, a slipway should be built at the side of the Promenade pier. The boat could be launched from there, except for about two hours at low water spring tides when the lifeboat from the Chapel station, which was about to be closed, could be moved to Skegness and operated from the existing boathouse. In September 1890 designs for a boathouse and slipway at the end of the pier were submitted, and a tender of £2,500 for a new boathouse was received. However, these plans proved to be unsuitable, and after a review the following month it was decided to look for a new site on the shore.

At the beginning of December 1890, the Inspector and the Rev R. W. Cracroft, of the Lincolnshire District Association, revisited the idea of a slipway and proposed one 160ft in length built parallel to the pier with a boathouse at its head, approached by a footway from the pier, which would cost approximately £1,000. However, this would have meant a second carriage-launched lifeboat was needed, and the Inspector believed that, if a carriage with spurs and Tipping's plates was provided, a second lifeboat and slipway would be unnecessary. In December 1890 a new carriage was

supplied by Lang, Howlett & Co, of Millwall, with Tipping's plates fitted over the main wheels to prevent them from sinking into soft sand. In October 1892 the lifeboat launched on exercise from the new carriage which enabled it to go almost 300 yards into the water without difficulty.

The new carriage improved matters, but the boathouse was still inadequate and so in 1892 plans were made for the construction of a new one. In June 1892 a tender of £640 was accepted from J. Crawshaw for removal of the existing lifeboat house and the building of a new one on the same site on the South Parade, with the agreement of the landowner, Lord Scarbrough. Work began later in the summer and by March 1893 the new lifeboat house was completed, at a cost of £679 1s 0d. Designed by Lewis & Duvivier, of London, the new building was larger and more imposing than that which it replaced, and doors were built at both ends so that the lifeboat could be taken in or out from either Drummond Road or South Parade. This house remained in use for more than a century, being altered and improved for subsequent lifeboats.

Ann, John and Mary's first service was on 8 April 1890 when she went to the sloop *Watson*, of Goole, which got into difficulties in very rough seas. Launching the lifeboat proved very difficult in the breaking seas, and many attempts had to be made before, after several hours of trying, the launchers succeeded in getting the lifeboat afloat. The four men on the sloop, initially reluctant to leave, were taken off and landed at 4am on 9 April.

In November 1893 *Ann, John and Mary* completed a very long service and was away from station for three days, putting into Sutton Bridge with the survivors of a Grimsby cod smack, and also stopping at Boston. The terrible gales of November 1893 wrecked many ships off Lincolnshire with great loss of life, and much wreckage was washed up on Skegness beach. The storm began on the morning of 18 November, and about midday on 19 November two vessels showing signals of distress were seen drifting south before wind and tide about two miles east of the station. The maroons were fired, and hundreds of people watched as the lifeboat, drawn by six horses belonging to

Ann, John and Mary on her carriage, possibly pictured during her formal inauguration into service. She was pulled by twelve oars and carried a crew of fifteen.

The lifeboat house completed in 1893 was used for almost a century with its front doors facing South Parade. It is pictured in June 1969 during the era of the motor lifeboats after various alterations had been made to it, including the lowering of the floor. (By courtesy of Grahame Farr)

Honorary Secretary Charles F. Grantham, launched. As Coxswain Thomas Smalley was ill, John Moody jnr, the Second Coxswain, took charge.

The lifeboat put out at 12.30pm to the cheers of the watching crowd. *Ann, John and Mary* and her crew battled the conditions, but it was a quarter of an hour before she made much headway through the surf. But once in open water, the sails were hoisted. The vessels had drifted a considerable distance south on wind and tide, and the lifeboat reached the first vessel, the schooner *Veda*, of Harwich, two hours after launching. The schooner's captain said that he was not in immediate danger and declined assistance, so the lifeboat made her way to the second vessel, the Grimsby cod smack *Frank* with seven crew, which was two miles further south. The vessel was disabled with masts and rigging blown away, having been hit by a huge wave. Some of the lifeboat crew boarded her to try to save her. The lifeboat stood by, but, when the weather worsened at about 4pm, those on the smack were taken off and the vessel was abandoned at the mouth of the river Nene.

The lifeboat took the survivors to Sutton Bridge, making for the Bridge Hotel, where survivors and lifeboat crew stayed the night. The crew was made up of Coxswain John Moody jnr, John Moody snr, William Green, John Green, Matthew Grunnill, William Grunnill, Amos Grunnill, Charles Grunnill, Joseph Grunnill, Montague Grunnill, Arkin Moody, Frank Moody, Thomas Hutson, Thomas Gillam and William Burrows. A steamer was needed to take the lifeboat back to Skegness but, as none were available the following day, the lifeboat did not return until 21 January.

While the lifeboat was stuck at Sutton Bridge, at about 3.30pm on 20 January some local fishermen reported that three ships were flying distress signals off the mouth of the Nene and that the lifeboat's help was required. Sutton Bridge is five miles from the sea and, with a gale blowing and no steamer available, it would have been impossible for the lifeboat to get out to sea had the landlord of the Bridge Hotel not provided his horse to tow the boat four miles down the river. But before the lifeboat reached them, the three vessels were helped by some Lynn smacks so the lifeboat headed back to Sutton Bridge. However, as the tide was now falling, the lifeboat grounded on the bar at the entrance to the river Nene at 7.30pm, where she remained stuck for six and a half hours. The crew were huddled in the boat throughout the night, facing the gale force winds and a raging sea.

The lifeboat crew eventually arrived back at the Bridge Hotel at 3.30am on 21 January, tired, cold and exhausted. However, the landlord, not expecting them to return, had let the beds they had occupied the previous night. He did provide a fire in the kitchen before which the crew soon fell asleep and, after breakfast later in the morning, they prepared for the journey home. They left Sutton Bridge at 9.30am and got across the upper reach of Boston Deeps but were so exhausted that they put into Boston for the night. On 22 January the lifeboat and her crew were towed home by a Boston steamer, reaching Skegness at 10am and being cheered by the large crowd which had come to see their return.

Ann, John and Mary had been away for three days and the crew had suffered much hardship during that time, but their deeds were immediately recognised by the local townsfolk who, only a few hours after the boat's return, entertained the crew to supper at a local hotel. It is difficult to imagine the hardships faced by the crew, without protection on their boat, during this long service and also how difficult it must have been to sail the lifeboat such distances in these conditions. The RNLI's account of the rescue did not include details of the difficult return passage, and it is perhaps surprising that no formal recognition was made to the lifeboat crew by the Institution for their exertions.

On 27 November 1897 a severe storm hit Skegness, with heavy rain accompanied by thunder and lightning, and storm force winds. About 4pm, a telegram was received from Hunstanton saying that a vessel was ashore on the Woolpack sands off the Norfolk coast, and asking the Skegness lifeboat to put out straight away. Despite the heavy seas, *Ann, John and*

Mary was soon afloat and, running with the wind and tide, made good progress towards the sandbank.

By the time she reached the Woolpack, it was very dark and huge waves were crashing over the sandbank. Coxswain Thomas Smalley realised that no vessel could survive for long in such conditions. The lifeboat was frequently engulfed by the heavy seas as she crossed the Woolpack, but the crew cleared the sands safely. On reaching smoother water, the lifeboat sailed up the coast towards Hunstanton and was then anchored for the night. The crew spent eight hours until dawn, contending with the rough seas and strong north-easterly wind, with the temperature almost down to freezing.

At dawn they continued to search, and eventually found a wreck but with only a small portion of the hull visible. Coxswain Smalley had little doubt that the vessel, the ketch *John Glee* of Blakeney, had gone down with all hands. The vessel had left Blakeney the previous day with a cargo of wheat and a crew of four, all of whom were drowned. As they were searching, the Skegness crew saw another lifeboat, which they took to be the Brancaster boat. So *Ann, John and Mary* returned to Skegness at midday after Coxswain and crew had been in rough seas for twenty hours. However, before they beached the lifeboat, the crew were sent to the assistance of a steamer, *Lydie Millington*, of Rostock, which was firing signals of distress off Gibraltar Point. However, on reaching the vessel it was found that the signals were for a pilot and the steamer, which had run out of coal, was awaiting a tow to Boston.

A few days after the loss of *John Glee*, a critical article appeared in the *St James Gazette* under the heading 'A Lifeboat Scandal. Four lives lost off Hunstanton'. The article explained how, on the previous Monday afternoon, at 2.30pm, the Hunstanton lookout at the lifeboat station saw a coaster aground on the Woolpack Sands seven miles away with the men in the rigging. The Skegness lifeboat, fourteen miles to windward of the wreck, was launched to help the stranded men, while the Brancaster boat was ordered to stand by. The Hunstanton lifeboat was ready for launching at 3pm but had no horses to take the boat across the beach.

Charles Fred Grantham, a distinguished townsman, served as Honorary Secretary from 1882 for forty years, being appointed to the post aged twenty-two. In 1902 he received an award from the RNLI for long and distinguished services. He was still holding the post at the time of his death in October 1922. Up to that time, the horses used to launch the lifeboats had usually come from his farms. (By courtesy of Skegness RNLI)

The Coxswain did not use his authority to requisition the necessary horses until twelve hours later, so the Hunstanton boat did not launch until 3am the next day.

A Board of Trade inquiry into the loss of the vessel opened at Hull on 11 January 1898, attended by, amongst others, Charles F. Grantham and Coxswain Thomas Smalley from Skegness. The problems of farmers supplying horses to the Hunstanton lifeboat were discussed, and the RNLI's Inspector, Commander Thomas Holmes RN, stated that the launching arrangements at that station were unsatisfactory. Mr Grantham said they had a team of eight horses at Skegness and had no difficulty launching, while had the message from Hunstanton arrived an hour earlier, the lifeboat would have arrived at the scene of the wreck before darkness. The action of the Skegness lifeboat was not questioned and the crew had performed their duty. A few weeks later, the court announced that the evidence showed every effort had been made by the lifeboat crews at Skegness and Hunstanton to get to the

ketch, but they were unfortunately too late to be able to help. Meanwhile, new arrangements were made for supplying horses at Hunstanton.

What proved to be the last service of *Ann, John and Mary* took place on 6 January 1905. Two of the lifeboat crew, Matt Grunnill (who became Coxswain in 1908) and Mont Grunnill, were out fishing in their small crab boat when they were caught in a north-westerly gale which broke the boat's mast. The fishing boat started to drift south, and the lifeboat launched soon after 3pm, with a large crowd manhandling boat and carriage into the water. The fishing boat was found before darkness and taken in tow, but became so waterlogged that it had to be cut adrift and its two occupants taken on board the lifeboat.

Samuel Lewis lifeboat

Shortly after this service, District Inspector Thomas Holmes recommended that, as most of the station's services were performed when the lifeboat was under sail and casualties were often

A fine photograph of Ann, John and Mary, the 37ft twelve-oared self-righter which served the station from 1888 to 1906. The high end-boxes, which gave the design the necessary buoyancy to self-right, are clearly visible. (By courtesy of Skegness RNLI)

some distance from the station, a sailing
lifeboat would be more suitable. This
recommendation was approved by the
RNLI's Committee of Management,
and in March 1905 a new lifeboat was
ordered for the station. The new boat was
appropriated to the gift of Mrs Ada Lewis-
Hill, of London, who had given £2,000
to the Institution to provide two lifeboats,
of which the Skegness boat was one. On
13 March 1905, in deciding on the most
suitable lifeboat, the local committee and
lifeboat crew requested a 35ft Liverpool
type boat be built for the station, and this
was ordered from the RNLI's boatbuilder
of the time, the Thames Ironworks, at
Blackwall, London.

The new lifeboat was ready in February
1906, and was named *Samuel Lewis* in
memory of the donor's first husband.

She was 35ft in length, 10ft in beam,
and fitted with double drop keels and a
yawl rig which gave the craft excellent
sailing qualities. She carried twelve oars,
which were used mainly when launching,
getting alongside a wreck, or in calm seas.
The Liverpool type was regarded as a
fine design of sailing lifeboat, especially
in difficult weather conditions, although
it was not self-righting and so would not
come upright in the event of a capsize.

Samuel Lewis arrived at Skegness on
29 March 1906, having been transported
free of charge from London via the Great
Northern Railway. A new carriage built by
the Bristol Wagon Works Co was brought
to the town by the Midland Railway. To
help launching, Tipping's plates, horse
launching poles and pushing poles were
also supplied. To accommodate the new

A rather blurred photo of
Samuel Lewis under sail.
She was fitted with a
standing forelug, jib and
standing mizen-lug. (By
courtesy of Joel Grunnill)

lifeboat, the doors at the front and rear of the boathouse were widened to 18ft by builder W. Crawshaw, at a cost of £42 2s 1d, and in 1909 a further £57 17s 10d was spent on improvements.

On 10 May 1906 the new lifeboat was taken out on exercise in an east-north-easterly moderate gale and very heavy seas and, according to the RNLI's minuted account, 'She behaved splendidly and the crew were perfectly satisfied with her'. With the arrival of the new lifeboat, the old lifeboat and carriage were condemned and, in April 1906, returned to the RNLI's storeyard in London. Unusually, on 14 June 1906, the old carriage was handed over to Margate to be used with the Surf Life Boat, a private venture, that was operated at the Kent town.

During more than twenty-six years at Skegness, *Samuel Lewis* launched twenty-one times, and is credited with saving the same number of lives. Her first effective service took place on 27 April 1907, when she launched at 9.30pm to the brig *Commerce*, of Great Yarmouth, which was stranded on the Knock Sand bound for Boston. Arriving on scene, the lifeboat went alongside and the Assistant Coxswain was transferred to the casualty. Efforts were then made to refloat the vessel, and at flood tide she was got off the sands.

On 11 July 1909, *Samuel Lewis* was again in action. During the evening, the ketch *Darnet*, of Maldon, anchored between the Knock and Main sandbanks, but her anchor parted and she drifted onto the sands. After the captain hoisted signals of distress, the lifeboat launched, and was soon alongside the ketch. The lifeboat stood by in case the vessel refloated at high water, but the vessel remained aground and eventually became a total wreck so the four crew were landed by the lifeboat.

The next service by *Samuel Lewis* took place more than three years later, on 31 October 1912, when she launched to the barge *Britannic*, of London. The barge, bound from Brightlingsea to Immingham Dock with a cargo of gravel, had been caught in a strong northerly gale. The lifeboat was launched in front of hundreds of people, and reached the barge two hours later. She then stood by until the steamer *Fox* arrived to take both the lifeboat and barge in tow, but because of the severity of the conditions the boat could not be beached safely and so made for Boston Dock, where she remained until the weather moderated. The lifeboat was towed back to Skegness the following day by another steamer, having been away from station for twenty-four hours.

Less than two weeks after this service, *Samuel Lewis* was involved in one of the station's most outstanding rescues. On

Samuel Lewis beaching prior to recovery. She was a non-self-righting lifeboat and, unlike her predecessor, had no large end boxes. (By courtesy of Skegness RNLI)

the morning of 13 November 1912, the Norwegian brig *Azha*, of Arendal, with her sails badly damaged in a gale, was seen off Sutton-on-Sea. At about 2.30pm, the vessel was seen on the Skegness Middle Sand and, as Coxswain Matthew Grunnill had anticipated that the lifeboat would be required, the crew and horses were ready and the boat was soon on her way. Due to the state of the tide, the lifeboat had to be taken to the Sea View, where several hundred people watched her launch.

At about 4.15pm the lifeboat, under oars, went alongside the stranded ship. A few minutes later signals were fired indicating assistance was required and a message was telegraphed to Boston for a tug. The 300-ton brig, bound for Shields with a cargo of pit-props, had been caught in a gale four days earlier which had considerably damaged her. Not only were her sails gone, but she was leaking and had taken on a lot of water. In the Humber a tug came to her assistance, but *Azha* twice broke loose and then drifted southwards.

Captain S. Salveson refused to abandon his ship, hoping the weather would improve, but her situation was hopeless as she was completely waterlogged. The crew could not go below deck, had had little warmth or food for four days, and been without sleep throughout. The lifeboat crew found them standing in the ice-cold water, so they were immediately taken off and made as comfortable as possible aboard the lifeboat. Coxswain Grunnill realised that nothing more could be done for the vessel, which was only afloat due to the timber cargo, and so he abandoned her. A couple of days later, she broke up and some of her cargo was washed ashore.

At Skegness, nothing more was seen of the lifeboat until 6.30pm, when news came through that she had come ashore two miles south and landed the rescued crew, six Norwegians and two Swedes. At 7pm, Coxswain Grunnill and his crew arrived at the boathouse and an hour later returned to recover *Samuel Lewis*. This proved a difficult task in the dreadful conditions, and the launchers were at times up to their waists in water as they got the boat back onto the carriage.

Although no formal recognition came from the RNLI, silver medals were awarded to Coxswain Grunnill and Second Coxswain Mont Grunnill by King Haakon of Norway for their part in a difficult rescue which saw the lifeboat arrive 'only just in time to avert a disastrous loss of life', according to the RNLI's account of the service in *The Lifeboat* journal of 1 May 1913. The rest of the crew received £20 from the King,

Samuel Lewis on her carriage, with the crew holding the oars for a posed photograph. (By courtesy of the RNLI)

which was divided amongst them. The other crew members who took part in this gallant service were Harry West, Matthew Henry West, William West, Charles Grunnill, William Grunnill, Hira Grunnill, Alfred Grunnill, Walter Grunnill, Francis Grunnill, Frank Moody, Charles Rose, Henry Rose, James Giles, Benjamin Major and William Burrows.

On 17 July 1915 *Samuel Lewis* was called on to help two vessels which were in difficulty. The fishing smack *Swan*, of Grimsby, and the barge *Harwich*, of Harwich, carrying 150 tons of shingle, stranded about three miles south-south-west of Gibraltar Point during a northerly gale with very heavy seas. As the smack appeared to be drifting before the gale, the Coastguard called out the lifeboat. When *Samuel Lewis* reached the vessels, the

A fine photo of Samuel Lewis sailing 'full-and-by', just off the pier head, with Coxswain Matt Grunnill (hidden by the lug mizzen) handling the boat. (By courtesy of the RNLI)

smack was aground, having sprung a bad leak, and the crew of four had abandoned the sinking vessel and boarded *Harwich*. Six of the lifeboat crew went aboard the barge to assist the already tired crew with the pumps and, on the flood tide, refloated her and got her into deep water. They remained with her until daylight, and then took her, with her three crew, to Boston. The four crew from the ketch were taken on board the lifeboat and landed ashore.

The other service undertaken during the First World War came on 26 February 1916 when *Samuel Lewis* was called to the 2,130-ton steamer *Bogatyr*, laden with iron ore, bound from Bilbao, Spain, to Middlesborough. The steamer went aground on the outlying sandbanks off Chapel St Leonards while battling her way up the east coast in a north-easterly gale. It was bitterly cold and mountainous seas were breaking over the vessel, which managed to fire a signal of distress. The weather was terrible, with a gale, rain and

sleet showers, and conditions were so bad on Skegness beach that the lifeboat had to be taken two miles north before a suitable place to launch could be found. Even then, when the boat was launched, the crew failed to keep her afloat and *Samuel Lewis* was driven ashore having taken a pounding in the surf, swamped more than once, and the oars whipped out of the crew's hands. The skilful seamanship of Coxswain Matthew Grunnill was all that prevented the lifeboat from capsizing.

The lifeboat was hauled back onto her carriage and then taken south of the pier, where over eighty soldiers, who were stationed at Skegness, pulled at a rope and hauled the lifeboat to the pier head so that finally she could get away. With her sails set, she arrived at *Bogatyr* an hour later and found three men on board, in a terrible condition. Of the twenty-three originally on board, Captain Nielsen and thirteen members of the crew had left earlier in one of the ship's lifeboats and landed at Chapel. Five more had also left in a boat, and drifted for more than twenty-one hours without fresh water before being picked up by another vessel and later landed at Immingham.

The four remaining men tried to get ashore in a small boat, but were unable to reach the shore and were lucky to reboard *Bogatyr*. They clung on at high water when the vessel was practically submerged, and a large sea swept away one of the Naval ratings. His body was later found on the beach, 300 yards north of the pier. At 3pm the three survivors were taken off by the lifeboat and landed at Skegness. For this outstanding service, Coxswain Grunnill was accorded the Thanks of the Institution Inscribed on Vellum.

The last effective service of *Samuel Lewis* took place on 30 August 1923 and was fairly routine in nature. She went to the fishing boat *Trixie*, which had broken from her moorings and was drifting out to sea. The lifeboat was launched at 11am in front of a crowd of holiday-makers, some of whom helped to get the boat down to the water. Once the lifeboat was afloat, her sails were hoisted and she made for the fishing boat. Nobody was on the vessel so three lifeboatmen went aboard, set the sails, and brought it safely ashore.

Although this was the last service in which she succeeded in assisting a casualty, *Samuel Lewis* remained on station for almost another decade and was involved in a number of ineffective services. She launched at 4.30am on 22

October 1924 in gale force winds to the spritsail barge *Royalty*, of Rochester, which had been driven ashore near Ingoldmells Point while bound for Hull with a cargo of sand. In the strong winds and heavy surf, the lifeboat crew were soaked as they pulled through the surf, and their boat was swept back almost to the pier before getting under way. However, their services were not needed, as the wreck was high and dry, and so *Samuel Lewis* returned to station and was recovered at 8.30am.

The crew of the stranded *Royalty*, a barge of eighty-four tons, were found at a cottage slightly to the north of the vessel. The skipper and his crew of two, who had all been supplied with dry clothes by the cottage's occupant, stated that the ship had been wrecked after the mainsails were damaged. The crew had all taken to the rigging, but eventually the water had fallen and the sea calmed sufficiently for

Samuel Lewis on her carriage being hauled by a team of six horses down South Parade from Tower Esplanade, with the pier in the background. (By courtesy of Joel Grunnill)

Samuel Lewis on her carriage being hauled across the beach by the station's first tractor, T15, which served from 1925 to December 1932. At the controls is Wilf Grunnill, the station's first tractor driver. (By courtesy of Skegness RNLI)

Samuel Lewis at oars off the pier. On board are, from bow to stern, on the starboard side, Bowman Frank Moody, Charles Rose, Acton Cumming, Bert Grunnill, Wilf Perrin, Bradbury, Alfred Grunnill, Coxswain Matthew Grunnill, and Second Coxswain Mont Grunnill. On the port side, bow to stern, are George Perrin, W. Burrows, George Steele, Ernest Grunnill, W. Perrin, and Harry Rose. (By courtesy of Skegness RNLI)

the crew to struggle ashore through about three feet of water.

The launch to the barge *Royalty* proved to be the last occasion when horses were used on a service launch as, by this time, the RNLI were beginning to use motor tractors at stations where carriage-launching was employed. The first trials with launching tractors had been held at Skegness' neighbouring station, Hunstanton, during the early 1920s, and their success led to more tractors being built throughout the decade.

In 1925 Skegness was supplied with its first tractor, a Clayton type, number T15. This tractor stayed until 1932 when T16, another Clayton, was sent to the station. The Clayton was the first motorised launch vehicle used by the RNLI, and eighteen were built between 1921 and 1927, including the two that served at Skegness. They offered considerable advantages over horses or manpower for hauling the lifeboat on its carriage over the beach, as they were more reliable and could move the boat more quickly.

Centenary Vellum

In May 1928, the RNLI's Committee of Management decided that every lifeboat station which had been operational for a century should be presented with a Centenary Vellum, and that a special ceremony of presentation should be organised. As this resolution was applied retrospectively, Skegness was eligible for such a certificate and was one of sixteen stations presented with a Vellum during the summer of 1928. The celebrations took place at the pier entrance on 13 August 1928, the same date as Lifeboat Day, when the Centenary Vellum Certificate was presented to the town in recognition of the service given since 1825.

Frederick Acton presided, and the Lord Lieutenant of Lincolnshire, the Earl of Yarborough, made the presentation on behalf of the RNLI. Yarborough gave a history of the station, paid tribute to the courage of the crews, and appealed to the public to show their appreciation of the contribution made by the Skegness lifeboatmen. He then presented the Vellum to Councillor G. E. Holmes, Chairman of the Council, and Councillor S. Moody, Chairman of the Branch. A further presentation, consisting of a framed print of a lifeboat setting out to rescue a stranded vessel, was also made on behalf of the Institution to Mr C. H. Major, proprietor and publisher of the *Skegness News*, to mark his valuable cooperation with the lifeboat station. The Vellum was signed by the Prince of Wales, and included details of the number of lives saved and medals awarded up to that date.

Anne Allen

A lthough the RNLI's first motor lifeboats saw service during the early 1900s, almost three decades passed before a suitable design of motor lifeboat was available for stations such as Skegness where carriage launching was employed. The first motor lifeboats were too large to be taken across a beach, and so were either kept afloat or launched down a slipway. The development of engines had not advanced enough for their power-to-weight ratio to be suitable for fitting into a relatively small lifeboat that could be manhandled on a beach and launched

from a carriage. With the First World War intervening to slow down the RNLI's motor lifeboat development programme, the first carriage-launched motor lifeboats did not enter service until the 1920s, and only in the 1930s were they being built in sufficient numbers for old pulling and sailing lifeboats to be systematically replaced in the RNLI's fleet.

The first motor lifeboat at Skegness, *Anne Allen*, was the second of a new class of single-screw Liverpool boats, one of two types designed to be launched from a carriage. She was similar in many respects to her predecessor, *Samuel Lewis*, and was

Anne Allen on trials on the river Thames shortly after being completed by J. I. Thornycroft at Chiswick. (By courtesy of the RNLI)

designed to retain the excellent qualities of the Liverpool type sailing boat but with the addition of an engine, which was housed in a cuddy amidships.

She was 35ft 6in in length with a beam of 10ft, fitted with a single drop-keel, a reduced yawl rig, and a 35hp six-cylinder Weyburn AE.6 engine which developed 3,300rpm. Two twenty-five gallon petrol tanks were carried below the deck, either side of the centre-plate, providing enough fuel to give the boat a radius of action of fifty-one nautical miles at her maximum speed of 7.2 knots. At her cruising speed of six and a half knots, with the propellers running at 730rpm, the radius of action increased to sixty-five miles.

Anne Allen, provided from the legacy of Mrs Anne Allen, of Spalding, had been built at a cost of £3,340 6s 6d by J. I. Thornycroft at Chiswick, the only Liverpool motor lifeboat built by the yard.

The new craft arrived at Skegness on Saturday 10 December 1932, having left Westminster Pier on the river Thames at about 7am on 8 December to head north. The RNLI's District Inspector for the east coast, Lieut Cdr P. E. Vaux, RN, was in charge during the passage, with three of the Skegness crew, Coxswain George Perrin, his son Wilfred Perrin, and Percy Grunnill, also part of the passage crew. A crew of eight was usually carried when the boat was on service.

The naming ceremony of the new boat took place on the Grand Parade, opposite the Pier Entrance, on Saturday 17 June 1933, in the presence of thousands of residents and visitors. Presiding for the occasion was Henry Haslam, MP. The lifeboat was presented to the station by the chairman of the RNLI's Committee of Management, Sir Godfrey Baring, and was received by Mr Haslam on behalf of the branch. The service of dedication was conducted by the Rev Canon Morris, Rector of Skegness. The Right Hon the Lord Yarborough, Lord Lieutenant and Vice-Admiral of Lincolnshire, then christened the boat. A vote of thanks was proposed by Walter Hudson, chairman of Skegness Urban District Council, and seconded by Honorary Secretary George Dunkley, after which the boat was launched for a short demonstration.

During her twenty-one years at Skegness, *Anne Allen* is credited with saving forty-three lives. She launched 120 times during that period, but the first two years of her career were relatively quiet, with only two launches. The first was on 23 April 1933, to a ditched aeroplane a mile and a half south of the pier, and the second on Christmas Day 1934 when she launched at 10.54pm to the steamship *Bella*, of Gothenburg. On neither occasion were her services needed, but her crew were at sea for more than three hours on the latter service, over Christmas night.

On 16 May 1935, *Anne Allen* undertook a very long service involving a round trip of eighty miles, partly under sail, although

she was not required to render any assistance to the casualty, the three-masted tramp steamer *Creek Fisher*, of Lancaster. The steamer was near the East Dudgeon lightship with her propeller gone, her rudder damaged, and heavy seas breaking over her. Hundreds of people braved biting winds on the beach to watch the launch at 10.25am, an extremely difficult one due to the surf and the state of the tide. The sixty-mile-an-hour northerly wind whipped the seas over the Burnham Flats so that passing through the channels leading eastwards was impossible. Coxswain Perrin therefore steered a course for the South Dowsing Buoy, crossing the broad channel eastward of the Docking.

The lifeboat continued on a south-easterly course until the disabled vessel was sighted and the low cliffs of the Norfolk coast were seen about nine miles to starboard. *Creek Fisher* had drifted out of control for nearly twelve miles from the position reported at 10am. A tug was standing by, waiting until the lifeboat had arrived before attempting the risky job of passing a line across. *Creek Fisher* signalled that she did not need lifeboat assistance, and a line was got across from the tug. Meanwhile, the Cromer lifeboat, *H. F. Bailey*, with Coxswain Henry Blogg in

command, had arrived and went alongside the Skegness boat. The assistance of neither was required as an offer from both boats to pass lines to the stern of *Creek Fisher* to assist in steering was declined, and shortly after 5pm the Skegness boat commenced her long journey homeward.

The crew expected to reach Skegness at about 9.30pm, but the engine broke down just before 7.30pm and Mechanic Percy Grunnill had to stop it immediately. The gale had moderated by this time, so the sails were set and the boat continued a slow passage towards her station; her crew had no food other than that in the emergency rations. They ran down the coast to beach at Skegness at about 7am and got the boat recovered. The lifeboat and her crew had been at sea for twenty-one hours, and this was the furthest any Skegness lifeboat had been called out.

On 19 August 1935, an unusual rescue took place off Skegness, but one which did not involve the lifeboat. The local motor pleasure cruiser *Elizabeth Allen* was on a routine trip with more than 100 people on board, including Joel Grunnill, when smoke began pouring from her engine. The lifeboat crew assembled immediately, but as it was a calm sea and several other boats were in attendance, the lifeboat was

Anne Allen and her crew on the beach in 1937. The crew are, from left to right, Bill Perrin, Percy Grunnill, Harold Steele, George Perrin, Mont Grunnill, Jack Soper, Acton Cumming and Lance Grunnill. (By courtesy of the RNLI)

not launched. Of the boats that went to the cruiser's aid, three were former RNLI lifeboats which had been converted into pleasure boats.

The first to reach the casualty was *Shamrock* skippered by Wilf Grunnill. By now, smoke was enveloping *Elizabeth Allen* and her master and engineer were trying to extinguish the fire. Some of the passengers were screaming, but Perrin took his boat alongside and took off sixty-eight of them, mostly women and children. Two other converted lifeboats, *Grace Darling II* (the former Coverack lifeboat) and *Skylark*, also went alongside, and took off the remainder of the passengers. By the time they had been landed, the fire on *Elizabeth Allen* had been extinguished and she was towed back. The RNLI presented an inscribed aneroid barometer to George Perrin for this rescue, and sent letters of thanks to Wilfred Grunnill and Hedley Grunnill, skippers of *Shamrock* and *Skylark* respectively.

The first effective service performed by *Anne Allen* took place on 2 December 1935. She launched at 11.32am to the 40ft fishing boat *Harold*, a fourteen-ton fishing smack with three Boston fishermen on board, which was showing distress signals six and a half miles south-east of Skegness. The cutter-rigged vessel left Boston on 30 November but got into trouble during a strong southerly gale. With the 15hp auxiliary motor breaking down, it was impossible to return to Boston, and the crew had no option but to ride out the storm. The anchor cable then parted, and the smack went ashore, where she remained throughout the night.

On 31 November, the vessel was refloated, but she was leaking badly and her crew were forced to man the pumps. The engineer managed to get the motor going, and they reached calmer water between the Outer Knock and Skegness. However, as *Harold* was taken to the Parlour Buoy, the motor stopped again. The crew spent the night soaked to the skin, working pumps to keep her afloat.

Lifeboat crew and station personnel with Anne Allen just before her first launch from Skegness. Standing in the boat are, left to right, Bob Grunnill, W. Perrin jnr, Jack Soper, Wilf Perrin snr, Mont Grunnill, Lance Grunnill, Percy Grunnill, Matt Grunnill, George Perrin, and the Coxswain and Second Coxswain of Runswick Bay lifeboat. (By courtesy of Joel Grunnill)

George Perrin, Coxswain from 1 April 1932 until 1947. Perrin had been a smacksman as a boy before serving in sailing and steam trawlers out of Grimsby, and served during the First World War as mate on trawler minesweepers. He joined the lifeboat crew in 1912, and was appointed Coxswain following a ballot of the crew. (By courtesy of the RNLI)

Anne Allen being recovered onto her carriage after exercise. (By courtesy of Terry Despicht)

Anne Allen being pulled out of the boathouse onto Drummond Road for an exercise by Case type L tractor T27. Head launcher Wilfred Grunnill is standing on the right, and behind him, near the stern of the boat, is Fred Miller. Jack Ramsden is driving the tractor. The three crew wearing caps in the stern of the boat are, left to right, Bill Perrin, Joel Grunnill and Percy Grunnill. The other two crew sitting and turning to face the camera are Bernard O'Reilly (on left) and Terry O'Reilly. (From an old postcard in the author's collection)

The next morning, with the wind freshening, the crew hoisted a distress signal and *Anne Allen* was launched, reaching the water's edge within eighteen minutes of the maroons being fired. In just over half an hour, the lifeboat had arrived on scene and found the fishing smack had drifted almost to the Lynn Knock light buoy. It was lying low in the water, wallowing heavily, and the crew were using buckets to bale the water. Coxswain Perrin skilfully put the lifeboat alongside, and as *Harold's* crew were too exhausted to jump, Second Coxswain Wilfred Perrin went aboard the sinking craft with a line which he made fast to hold the lifeboat in place while the three men were transferred. The lifeboat's crew had to haul them over the smack's rail and into the lifeboat, after which Second Coxswain Perrin cast off the line and jumped back into the lifeboat. The smack was so waterlogged that it was impossible to salvage her, and she sunk shortly after the lifeboat had left her.

The next service by *Anne Allen* was on 19 June 1936, when she went to the small yacht *F. L. B.*, of Blyth, which was aground on the Outer Knock, three miles south-west of the pier. The lifeboat was launched at 4.25pm and reached the scene to find the yacht's two crew, who were taking the vessel on a delivery voyage to Pin Mill, exhausted and unsure of their position. The lifeboat towed the craft clear, gave her the course for Cromer and then made for home. The yacht soon signalled again for help, however, and so the lifeboat returned and escorted her to Wainfleet Haven.

During summer, if the lifeboat was called out, the launch would often be witnessed by holiday-makers who came to the resort, and on 7 August 1936 large numbers of visitors watched *Anne Allen* as she launched for a routine service. She went to the assistance of the small yacht *Madeline*, which was flying distress signals two and a half miles south-east of Skegness. The yacht, bound from Dover to Bridlington, was taken in tow by the lifeboat to Gibraltar Point. Owing to the state of the tide, both vessels had to wait five hours for high water before they could enter the haven.

Anne Allen on exercise on 11 November 1951. On board, from left to right, are: Morris Hatton, Ken Holland, Aubrey Patrick, Lance Grunnill, Joel Grunnill (partially hideen), Percy Grunnill, Bernard O'Reilly, and Don Bullen. (By courtesy of Joel Grunnill)

Far fewer people were on the beach to watch the lifeboat launch on 26 January 1937 to the 1,300-ton coaster *Olavus*, bound from the Tyne to Boston in ballast, which had gone ashore on the Dogs Head in the early hours of the morning. *Anne Allen's* crew found *Olavus* high and dry on the sands, so Coxswain George Perrin beached the lifeboat on the western edge of the sand and some of the lifeboatmen went ashore and walked, for more than a mile in sea boots and oilskins, to the ridge where the vessel was lying. The Captain asked the lifeboatmen to return to Skegness and send a message to the vessel's owners. They sent a message using semaphore to coastguards on the pier and then, with *Olavus* about to refloat unaided, the lifeboat returned to station.

On 17 November 1937, the spritsail barge *Britannic* got into difficulty while making her way along the North Norfolk coast towards Wells-next-the-Sea. Manned by a crew of three, the 148-ton steel-built sailing barge passed Cromer in the early hours and headed for Wells with a strong easterly gale behind her. She was off Wells before daylight, somewhere around 6am, but the bar was too dangerous to cross, so the master, in the darkness, decided to await an improvement in conditions. However, at 8.30am, the barge struck the sand, her rudder was torn away and her aft compartment breached. Thus disabled and leaking, she drove over the sand and

dropped anchor before reaching more dangerous, deeper water. Her crew, after stopping the leaks, hoisted signals of distress which were seen aboard the Lynn Well lightship, whose look-outs passed the message to the coastguards.

Anne Allen was launched at once and, despite low water making conditions far from ideal, was quickly on her way. At 1.15pm, an hour and a half after launching, she came alongside the barge,

Anne Allen at sea in icy conditions in winter 1947, one of the coldest of the twentieth century in the British Isles. Snowfall was heavy and snow cover persisted from late January to mid March. The four crew pictured are, left to right, Percy Grunnill, Joel Grunnill, Bernard O'Reilly and Lance Grunnill. (By courtesy of Joel Grunnill)

Eight shire horses belonging to local farmer J. K. Measures were used to recover Anne Allen on 24 February 1936. As the tractor was launching the boat two days earlier, the vehicle's clutch failed. The lifeboat managed to get away, but the tractor and carriage were stuck and subsequently covered by the tide. The following day, the horses managed to get the carriage clear, and then recovered the boat which had been moored at Gibraltar Point for two days. The tractor was also eventually hauled out by the horses. This was the final time horses were involved in lifeboat work, having last been used ten years previously. The tractor, T16, was repaired, but replaced the following year. (By courtesy of Joel Grunnill)

which was riding at anchor in the lee of the Middle Bank. Getting the lifeboat alongside was difficult, but once this was accomplished some lifeboatmen went aboard and assisted the crew in salvaging their personal belongings. Shortly after 1.30pm, with the survivors and their dog safely aboard, the lifeboat headed for Skegness. After a rough nine-and-a-half mile passage, she was beached shortly after 3.15pm. A tug was sent from King's Lynn the following day, found *Britannic* still riding at anchor, and towed her to King's Lynn for repairs. Coincidentally, twenty-five years previously, on 31 October 1912, *Samuel Lewis* had launched to render assistance to the same vessel.

On 23 November 1938, during a south-westerly gale when at times the wind gusted to 70mph, two coastguard officers on watch at the pier head spotted a drifter, the Boston-registered *Dusty Miller*, carrying a crew of three, flying a distress signal. The maroons were fired just before

2pm and, despite the gale, and the fact that it was low water, *Anne Allen* was afloat within fourteen minutes. Another vessel, the coaster *Rudderman*, of London, was standing by the drifter when the lifeboat reached the scene shortly before 3pm. The coaster had been trying to rescue the drifter's crew by streaming lifelines.

As the lifeboat approached, the drifter was lying low in the water with seas breaking right over her. *Rudderman* was lying head to sea between the drifter and the shore, and her master then steamed steadily south to give the lifeboat a lee as she came alongside the casualty. With their ship sinking, the crew of *Dusty Miller* were ready to leave and, as the lifeboat came alongside, the three men jumped across. The lifeboat then sheered off, and headed for station with the rescued men and was beached at 4.05pm. The survivors were taken ashore and given hot baths, a warm fire and meals.

The war years

During World War II, *Anne Allen* and her crew were kept busy searching for crews from crashed aircraft, both Allied and German, that had ditched in the Wash and the North Sea. The lifeboat crew were sometimes called out two or three times a week, and spent hours at sea often in appalling weather with little protection searching. On 30 September 1940 *Anne Allen* was launched to search for an aircraft reported in the sea off Hunstanton, but despite covering nearly fifty miles throughout the night, the crew did not find anything. However, about midnight, they realised they were in a

Painting displayed in the lifeboat house showing Anne Allen on service to the drifter Dusty Miller, of Boston, and her crew of three on 23 November 1938.

minefield, as it was low water and the mines were visible. Coxswain George Perrin proceeded slowly and managed to get the lifeboat out of danger, anchoring until dawn, and then searching in daylight. The lifeboat was at sea for thirteen hours, but found no trace of any wreckage.

In the early hours of 28 October 1940 a bomber got into difficulties and crashed within 200 yards of the pier. Coastguards heard cries for help from the airmen, who were struggling in the water, and the lifeboat was called. When the boat on her carriage reached the end of Tower Esplanade, the soldiers were reluctant to open the barbed wire barricades which prevented the public from reaching the beach, and it took Coxswain George Perrin some time to get the authorities to let the lifeboat through. After a considerable delay, the lifeboat eventually launched and, using searchlights, found the airmen. One was afloat, and he was brought ashore by the lifeboatmen, but despite going to Skegness Hospital, he did not respond to treatment and sadly died soon afterwards. The other three were all drowned and the bodies later washed up.

On 9 January 1942 the London tug *Arcadia* and the steamer *Eastwood*, which was being towed north for repairs, went ashore on the Burnham Flats. Both were damaged, and *Anne Allen* launched to their assistance. The Wells lifeboat *Royal Silver Jubilee 1910-1935* also arrived on scene, and both lifeboats stood by until 1.30am when another large tug arrived. It was a bitterly cold night and the crews of both

lifeboats had very little protection from their small canopies. On arriving back at Skegness, George Perrin reported the circumstances to naval officers who sent for another tug from the Humber and the next day both vessels were taken in tow.

During 1943 and 1944 *Anne Allen* undertook further services to aircraft. On 21 January 1943 she launched during the late morning after two planes, a Lysander and a Spitfire, collided south of the pier.

Anne Allen entering the water prior to being launched, with Joel Grunnill at the stern, and crew member Harold Steele on the right. (By courtesy of Joel Grunnill)

Anne Allen launching off the beach through the surf, with Jack Ramsden driving the tractor and Wilf Grunnill standing between boat and tractor. (By courtesy of Joel Grunnill)

Lifeboat crew and station officials gather on the beach with Anne Allen. Standing in the boat are, left to right, Terry O'Reilly, Ken Holland, Bernard O'Reilly, Aubrey Patrick, Bill Perrin, Joel Grunnill, Percy Grunnill and George Perrin. Standing are, left to right, S. Major, T. Kiss, Mick Sumner, A. Blanchard, B. Holman, Fred Miller, Len Cant, unknown, Wilf Grunnill, Bert Hydes, Phil Holvey and Jack Ramsden. (By courtesy of RNLI Skegness)

The lifeboatmen picked up two bodies from the Lysander, but they could not find the Spitfire and returned to station. On 27 June 1943 she launched to search for survivors from an aeroplane which had crashed into the sea off Chapel. The lifeboatmen found two survivors in a dinghy, one with a broken spine and the other with injured legs. A third was in the water attached to the dinghy by a line, but he was dead. The two survivors and the body were taken ashore, and dinghies and some of the gear was also landed.

The next incident involving an aircraft took place on 25 July 1944, after a Lancaster bomber went down six miles from Anderby Creek. The aircraft had a bomb jammed in the bomb rack so the pilot attempted to land at sea, close to the shore. But when the aircraft hit the water, the bomb exploded, killing all the occupants and blowing the plane to pieces. The aircraft could be seen on fire when the lifeboat put out at 5.28am and, about eight miles from Skegness pier, the lifeboatmen found some wreckage but, despite a large search, no survivors. They picked up various items, but nobody survived and a few days later the bodies of the airmen were found on the beach.

One of the longer services of the war took place on 20 and 21 August 1944. Just before 8pm on 20 August the coastguard

reported that the Hull steamer *VIC 72*, in ballast, was in difficulties south of Skegness pier. *Anne Allen* launched at 9.35pm into a north-easterly gale with rough seas and driving rain. The steamer had lost her bearings and her engine had broken down. The lifeboat crew guided her to the calmer waters of Boston Deeps, took on board two of her five crew who were suffering from exposure, and landed them at 12.15am on 21 August. At 6.45am the lifeboat went out again, with a pilot on board. The pilot and two lifeboatmen went aboard the steamer, which the lifeboat then escorted into Boston. *Anne Allen* was back on station at 9.05am.

Post-war service

The first notable service after the war was to the Boston fishing smack *Virginia*, which had been missing in the Wash for three days in January 1947. The smack's crew had anchored near the Dogshead Sand after the vessel's engine had broken down. With the weather worsening, considerable anxiety was felt in Boston for the fishing smack. On 5 January, three days after the vessel had been reported missing, the fishermen, in desperation, ignited petrol-soaked bags to attract attention, and fortunately the light was spotted by Coxswain George Perrin who ordered the lifeboat to be launched. *Anne*

Anne Allen and her launching tractor on display on the Grand Parade, just north of the Clock Tower, summer 1951. The chalkboard hanging from her bow describes her last service, which was saving a dinghy and six lives in June 1951. (By courtesy of RNLI Skegness)

Allen found *Virginia* six miles south-east of Skegness pier, with a tanker standing by, so towed the craft to Boston. A meal was cooked for the lifeboatmen by the smack's owner, after which the lifeboat returned to Skegness to be recovered and rehoused.

During 1950, *Anne Allen* had one of her busiest years. On 28 June, she launched in choppy seas to help a rubber dinghy in difficulty off the North Shore, and saved three women, a young girl and two men from the craft. The following day, at 9.58pm, she went to a sailing boat that was drifting out to sea near Chapel Point. The boat's engine had broken down but, by the time the lifeboat arrived, it was working again so the vessel only needed escorting.

On 17 July, two boys were swept out to sea in a rubber dinghy off Chapel St Leonards beach. One jumped overboard and reached the shore, while the other stayed in the dinghy. *Anne Allen* launched at 2pm and picked up the boy three miles north of Chapel Point. As the lifeboat headed for station, a radio-telephone message was received stating that the boy's father was adrift in an inflated motor tube having swum out to search for the second boy. After a search by the lifeboat, the father was found, unconscious, picked out of the makeshift craft, and brought ashore.

The final service of the year came on 7 October when *Anne Allen* launched at 10.36pm to a vessel reported in danger near the Lynn Well lightvessel. She found the yacht *Catriona*, of Littlehampton, with her engine broken down. The lifeboat

towed the yacht to Boston, and then on her way back to Skegness the crew spotted the body of a fisherman which was recovered and landed ashore.

During her last three years at Skegness, *Anne Allen* performed one service a year, all somewhat routine affairs. On 10 July 1951, she launched at 7.10pm after reports that a rubber dinghy with six people in it was drifting out to sea at Ingoldmells Point. The dinghy was found two and a half miles north-north-east of Skegness pier, and the lifeboat took on board two men, three women and a boy, and returned to station an hour and a half after launching. On 18 April 1952, two RAF Sabre aeroplanes collided, so the lifeboat launched and found one of the pilots in a rubber dinghy about three miles off Gibraltar Point. He was picked up and transferred to an air-sea rescue launch.

The lifeboat's final service took place on 27 October 1953 after the crew of a Trinity House vessel reported seeing red flares south-west of North Race Buoy.

Anne Allen shortly after being sold out of service. She was used as a fishing boat for a number of years. (By courtesy of Terry Despicht)

Anne Allen as the angling boat Golden Fleece II. She was kept in Blakeney Pit during the summer, but moved to Great Yarmouth in winter. (Nicholas Leach)

Anne Allen at Sutterton undergoing restoration under the supervision of owner Terry Despicht. (Nicholas Leach)

Anne Allen launched at 7.10am into rough seas and stood by the motor barge *Will Everard*, of London, anchored at the north end of the Burnham Flats. Her steering gear had broken, and the steamer *Arthur Wright*, which found the barge, took it in tow to Great Yarmouth.

A couple of months after this incident, *Anne Allen* left Skegness for the last time, to be replaced by another 35ft 6in Liverpool motor lifeboat. During her two decades at the station she had given sterling service and proved her worth during many difficult services, particularly during the war. After leaving Skegness on 8 December 1953, she was taken

to Leo Robinson's boatyard at Oulton Broad, Lowestoft, by a crew made up of Second Coxswain Joel Grunnill, Second Mechanic Lance Grunnill and an RNLI mechanic. From there, she was sold out of service to the company of G. H. Cox, a fishing family of Wells-next-the-Sea, and converted into a whelker. She was a popular boat with the fishermen because of her good sea-keeping abilities and worked off the North Norfolk coast for the best part of two decades.

In the early 1970s she was laid up ashore for a number of years before being purchased by Stratton Long Marine, of Blakeney. She was again modified, this time being converted into an angling party boat, and bought by Michael 'Tickie' Taylor who took groups of anglers from the Blakeney estuary in summer and out of Great Yarmouth in winter. She had by this time been renamed *Golden Fleece II*. In December 1999, poor health forced Michael to sell the boat and she was purchased by Terry Despicht. Having discovered she was a Lincolnshire lifeboat, he decided that restoring her would be a worthwhile if challenging task. She was moved to Sutterton in 2001, and a complete restoration began so she could go afloat again looking as close to her original lifeboat appearance as possible.

The Cuttle

On 7 December 1953, another single-engined 35ft 6in Liverpool type boat, *The Cuttle*, arrived at Skegness to replace *Anne Allen*, which, after more than twenty years on station, was beginning to show her age. Although not new, this boat was younger than *Anne Allen*, having been built in 1940 as one of only a handful of lifeboats completed during the war.

While *Anne Allen* was the second single-engined Liverpool motor, *The Cuttle* was the penultimate boat of the class, of which a total of twenty-eight were built. Some changes were made to the design during the build programme, with the beam increased to 10ft 3in for the last nineteen boats of the class, and *The Cuttle* was thus slightly beamier than the boat she replaced. Before the boat was sent to Skegness, Honorary Secretary T. Kiss, Coxswain Wilfred Perrin and Mechanic Percy Grunnill visited Filey to inspect the boat, which was completely overhauled before coming to her new station.

Like *Anne Allen*, *The Cuttle* was powered by a single 35hp Weyburn AE.6 six-cylinder petrol engine which developed 3,300rpm, gave her a top speed of 7.38 knots and a range of fifty-one nautical

35ft 6in Liverpool motor lifeboat The Cuttle on her launching carriage on the Promenade. (By courtesy of the RNLI)

The Cuttle inside the boathouse, 29 March 1959. (Jeff Morris)

The Cuttle being launched on exercise off the beach with Ron Chapman watching from the beach. (By courtesy of Joel Grunnill)

miles. At her cruising speed of seven knots, she had a range of fifty-six nautical miles; a total of forty-eight gallons of fuel were carried. Built at Groves & Guttridge yard in Cowes, she was funded from the legacy of Miss F. L. Cuttle, of Rotherham. She was never formally christened due to wartime restrictions and spent the first thirteen years of her career at Filey, where she is credited with saving twenty-eight lives. The most notable visual difference between *The Cuttle* and her predecessor

were the Sampson posts, of which *The Cuttle* had two, just abaft of the bow end box, while *Anne Allen* had one.

Although originally intended as something of a temporary measure until a new lifeboat had been built, *The Cuttle* served at Skegness for just over a decade during which time she launched almost fifty times on service and is credited with saving eleven lives. Her first service took place on 18 July 1954, and was a routine incident. She launched at 9.50pm to the

A sequence of photos showing The Cuttle beaching and being recovered on Easter Sunday, 15 April 1963. She was returning from service after launching to a bather who got into difficulties off Mablethorpe. She was recalled after the bather was brought safely to shore by others. In the bottom photo, Coxswain Wilf Perrin is standing by the lifeboat's keels. (Jeff Morris)

The Cuttle on her carriage after being recovered on 15 April 1963. She had launched on service to a bather in difficulties. Tractor T43, a Case LA type, was on station at this time. (Jeff Morris)

Lifeboat crew line up in front of The Cuttle on the beach. They are, left to right, Bert Hydes, Wilf Grunnill, Phil Holvey, Herbert Sharpe, Len Cant, Don Bulen, Titch Holman, Fred Miller, Mick Sumner, Bernard O'Reilly, Aubrey Patrick, Terry O'Reilly, Joel Grunnill, Percy Grunnill, Bill Perrin and William Bosworth (foreshore manager for the council). (By courtesy of Skegness RNLI)

converted ship's boat *Venture*, which had two people on board and was fitted with an auxiliary engine. The engine had broken down so the boat was towed to Wainfleet Haven by the lifeboat, which returned to station at 3am on 19 July.

During 1956, *The Cuttle* performed two services. The first was on 29 July to the yacht *Vagabond*, of Peterborough, which had broken down and needed help. The lifeboat launched at 2.40am and, after a short search, found the yacht with two crew on board. She then towed the yacht to Wainfleet Haven, where the vessel was beached. The other service, on 29 August, proved to be a rather tragic incident. At 4.35pm the coastguard reported a bather being washed out to sea north of the pier. The lifeboat launched at 5pm, and searched the area with a helicopter. Eventually the body of a girl was found 200 yards off shore so it was picked up and brought back to the station.

Further services during the latter years of the 1950s were also somewhat routine affairs. At 2.50pm on 12 July 1958, *The Cuttle* launched to help a man whose dinghy had capsized 500 yards from the shore, two miles north of the pier. The lifeboat saved the man and brought him ashore, together with his dinghy. On the evening of 27 September she went to the cabin cruiser *Olivier*, which needed help off Skegness. The vessel, whose American owner was on board, had engine trouble and so was towed to Wainfleet Haven.

On 29 July 1959 *The Cuttle* launched at 5.30am to pick up four survivors from the motor vessel *Rivergate*, of Hull, who were on the Inner Dowsing lightvessel. Their vessel, on passage to Goole, had grounded off Lowestoft, refloated, but then started leaking as she made her way north. The crew had taken to an inflatable dinghy and managed to reach the lightvessel. On 4 October 1959, the lifeboat towed the fishing boat *Our Boys*, and its crew of two and a dog, to a safe anchorage in Wainfleet Haven after the fishing boat started leaking and the engine became flooded.

On 17 June 1961, at 5.30pm, *The Cuttle* launched to search for the 12ft motor boat *Bluebelle*, which had been seen three hours earlier heading north but with only enough fuel to last an hour. Two RAF helicopters and another local boat joined in the search,

which proved fruitless, even though Coxswain Perrin and his crew searched throughout the night, taking their boat out into the darkness beyond the Inner Dowsing lightvessel. The lifeboat returned to station at 5am on 18 June having been at sea for twelve hours.

The following day, an RAF Valletta aircraft continued to scour the area until, at 4.05pm, a message was received stating that the motor boat, with a boy on board, had been picked up by the Swedish steamship *Stallaria* after the boat had been spotted tied up to a buoy five miles south-south-west of the Dowsing lightvessel. At 4.50pm the lifeboat launched with a doctor on board, picked the boy up from the steamer, and returned him to Skegness

Lifeboat crew on board The Cuttle at sea. From left to right: Terry O'Reilly, Philip Lill, Percy Grunnill, Ken Holland, Lance Grunnill, Bill Perrin, Stanley Major, Bernard O'Reilly, and (at back) unknown. (Joel Grunnill)

Coxswain Wilfred Perrin with Honorary Secretary Frank Janney. Perrin joined the crew in 1921, and became Second Coxswain in 1934 before being promoted to Coxswain in 1947. A year before his retirement in 1965, he brought Charles Fred Grantham to Skegness. Janney served in his post from 1955 to 1965 and, on his retirement, was presented with a pair of binoculars by Cdr H. P. F. Grenfell, a vice-president of the Institution. (By courtesy of the RNLI)

The Cuttle during a courtesy visit to the Lynn Well lightvessel to deliver Christmas gifts to the vessel's crew. For many years Skegness lifeboats made an annual trip at Christmas time to the Lynn Well lightvessel, which for over 150 years, marked the channels to King's Lynn and Boston before being replaced with a light buoy in 1973. (By courtesy of Joel Grunnill)

where his parents were awaiting him. He had spent twenty-four hours in the 12ft speedboat after his motor had failed to restart, half a mile from the shore at Anderby Creek. When picked up the following day, he was twenty-one miles north-east of Anderby.

Many launches by *The Cuttle* were to help pleasure craft, bathers, dinghies and inflatables. Indeed the last service she performed while at Skegness, on 9 September 1963, was to two dinghies, one of which had capsized off Jackson's Corner. The lifeboat launched at 12.40pm

and within an hour had picked up three men and the dinghies, which had drifted two miles off Vickers Point by the time they were reached. A helicopter was also called, and it circled the two dinghies until the lifeboat reached them. The lifeboat returned to station at 4.30pm, and one of the boats' owners sent a donation to RNLI funds together with a letter of appreciation for the lifeboat's services.

In April 1964, *The Cuttle* was replaced as Skegness lifeboat. After leaving Skegness, she was placed in the Reserve Fleet for a couple of years until being sold out of service in April 1966 from Robinson's Boatyard at Oulton Broad, near Lowestoft. She was converted into a yacht, but while bound from London for Gibraltar in October 1967 caught fire and sank near the Île d'Oléron off France. Her crew of three were saved by a sea rescue

patrol boat, and, although she was later beached, she subsequently became a wreck and was abandoned.

Inshore Lifeboats

The growth of the leisure industry during the 1950s saw an increasing number of people using the sea for recreation, and consequently more people were getting into difficulty, often within sight of land and in moderate weather. In response to

The Cuttle being pulled down Tower Esplanade for launching, probably during a lifeboat day in the early 1960s, by tractor T43, a Case LA type built in 1948. (By courtesy of the RNLI)

The station's first inshore lifeboat, No.15, being put through her paces off the beach. (By courtesy of Skegness RNLI)

Two photographs showing the first Skegness inshore lifeboat, No.15, in the temporary compound, 18 April 1965, a few days after the boat had been delivered to the station for the summer season. At this time, she was kept in a council yard, not far from where the present boathouse was subsequently built. The boat was 15ft 3in in length and powered by a 40hp Evinrude outboard. (Jeff Morris)

the increasing number of inshore incidents such as the one described above, the RNLI introduced a new rescue tool – the inshore rescue boat (IRB), later designated inshore lifeboat (ILB) – in 1963. Conventional lifeboats were not well suited to dealing with inshore incidents, where speed was of the essence, so the IRB, a small, fast rescue craft, was developed.

The RNLI bought its first inflatable boat in 1962 for extensive trials, and a delegation visited France, where similar boats were in operation. The first IRBs were introduced during the summer of 1963 at ten stations, and such was their success that more and more places operated the boats in subsequent years. The inflatable lifeboats, 15ft to 16ft in length, were made from tough nylon with neoprene, could be launched quickly and easily and were manned by two or three crew. Their speed of twenty knots was considerably faster than any lifeboat in service during the early 1960s, and they could go alongside other craft or persons in the water without causing or suffering damage.

In May 1964, inshore rescue boat No.15 was sent to Skegness, a 15ft 6in RFD PB16 type. The boat was kept behind the lifeboat house on Drummond Road in temporary accommodation until a permanent home was found on the seafront, on Tower Esplanade, in a separate boathouse completed in April 1966. The crew was drawn from a rota of six or seven suitably trained men. This craft was also provided with its own tractor to take it to the water's edge.

The first launch by the new IRB took place on 28 June 1964, but her services were not needed. The first effective service came on 19 July 1964, when she went to a sailing dinghy which had capsized a mile north-east of Skegness. The IRB put out at 2.38pm, took the dinghy in tow, beached her north of the pier, and brought the three people on board to safety. Although the IRB did not perform any further services during her first season, the following year another IRB was sent to the station, D-58, and inflatable lifeboats have been in service ever since. D-58 she remained on station until the end of the summer season in 1972.

Charles Fred Grantham

In April 1964, a new 37ft Oakley type lifeboat, *Charles Fred Grantham*, was sent to Skegness. The Oakley type, designed by and named after the RNLI's Consulting Naval Architect Richard Oakley, was 37ft in length, had a beam of 11ft 6in, and was manned by a crew of seven or eight. The Oakley's hull was of wood and the boat was suitable for carriage launching across beaches.

Developed during the mid-1950s, it was the first lifeboat design to have a high degree of inherent stability and also self-right in the event of a capsize. Self-righting was achieved through an ingenious water ballast system which transferred 1.54 tons of water ballast into a righting tank on the port side to right the boat. During trials, righting took about six seconds from the overturned position to the boat being upright. Her weight of just over nine tons when on her carriage increased to more than eleven tons when afloat with her water-ballast tank full.

Power came from twin Parsons Porbeagle four-cylinder diesels of 52bhp each, which gave a maximum speed of 8.21 knots, with the engine running at 1,003rpm, consuming 4.49 gallons per hour, and giving a range of eighty-seven nautical miles. At her cruising speed of seven knots, fuel consumption was 2.09 gallons per hour and the boat's range increased to 160 nautical miles. She carried ninety-six gallons of fuel. Built at Groves & Guttridge boatyard at Cowes on the Isle of Wight, the RNLI's builder of the time, *Charles Fred Grantham* headed for Skegness in April 1964.

She left Cowes on 18 April under the charge of Cdr L. F. L. Hill, Inspector for the North-Eastern District, together with four crew from Skegness, Coxswain Wilfred Perrin, Mechanic Percy Grunnill, Bowman Ken Holland and John B. Strzelecki. Accompanying the boat was W. Witkowski, of Orby, secretary of the Spilsby financial branch. The boat stayed at Dover overnight on 18 April and at Gorleston on 19 April. On 20 April, she passed the north Norfolk coast and made the passage through the Sledway and across the Wash approaches to reach Skegness at 2.24pm.

The 37ft Oakley class lifeboat Charles Fred Grantham as built, with an open aft cockpit, no radar and a grey-painted engine casing.

Amongst those awaiting her arrival was Richard Oakley, MRINA, the RNLI's Surveyor of Lifeboats, and the designer after whom the type was named. To enable the new boat to be accommodated, the boathouse floor was lowered by about ten inches. The house had already been extended for *Anne Allen*, and the house was extended at the back by about 4ft.

The boat's £34,000 cost was defrayed from the legacies of Mrs Elizabeth Wright Montford, of Market Drayton, and Miss Mary Dearden, of Hyde, Cheshire, and the RNLI asked the Skegness committee to suggest a name which would commemorate a well-known personality or geographical location from or around Skegness. The name *Charles Fred Grantham* was proposed by the then

vice-chairman of the lifeboat committee, Lt Cdr F. S. W. Major, RNVR, and was approved by the committee. Charles Fred Grantham was a distinguished townsman, the first chairman of the Urban Council, and Honorary Secretary at the station for forty years, from 1882 to 1922.

The new lifeboat was named at a ceremony on 9 July 1964 at Skegness pier. F. S. W. Major opened proceedings and Cdr L. F. L. Hill, District Inspector, described the new boat. The Earl of Scarbrough, whose family had been involved in the development of Skegness as a resort and who was president of the Branch, formally presented the lifeboat to the RNLI, and she was accepted by Rear-Admiral Robert St Vincent Sherbrooke, a member of the Committee

Charles Fred Grantham arriving at Skegness for the first time after her passage from Groves & Guttridge's yard in Cowes, April 1964. (By courtesy of Joel Grunnill)

Charles Fred Grantham is recovered at Skegness for the first time, April 1964. Kneeling on the bow is Ken Holland, while Wilf Perrin is behind him with one leg over the side. (By courtesy of Joel Grunnill)

Charles Fred Grantham is hauled onto the beach at Skegness for the first time, April 1964. (By courtesy of Joel Grunnill)

Preparing to launch Charles Fred Grantham for the first time, April 1964, on the day she arrived at Skegness. The Case 1000D tractor T75, supplied for the Oakley, was on station from 1964 to 1966. (By courtesy of RNLI Skegness)

of Management. Frank Janney accepted the boat on behalf of the station.

The service of dedication was led by the Right Rev Anthony Otter, Bishop of Grantham, assisted by three other members of the clergy. A statuette of a lifeboatman was presented to Admiral Sir Guy Grantham, CBE, DSO, son of the former Honorary Secretary and a former NATO Commander-in-Chief, by Mrs George Perrin on behalf of the Institution. After the formalities, a vote of thanks was proposed by Councillor F. A. Wise, chairman of Skegness Urban District Council, and Admiral Grantham christened the new boat *Charles Fred Grantham* in honour of his father.

The first service carried out by *Charles Fred Grantham* took place on 3 May 1964, a couple of weeks after she had arrived on station and just over two months before her naming ceremony. She launched at

12.15pm to a catamaran that had been
dismasted half a mile off Winthorpe and
was drifting northwards. A dinghy also
went to help the catamaran, but was blown
out to sea as well, so the lifeboat towed the
dinghy, catamaran, and their respective
crews back to the beach. Her other service
of 1964 came on 2 November when she
landed two men and two boys who were
stranded on the Inner Dowsing lightvessel.

During 1965, *Charles Fred Grantham*
completed five effective services, and
saved a number of lives. She landed a man
in need of urgent dental treatment from
the Lynn Well lightvessel on 15 January,
and on 19 April launched to the sloop *Hal
o' the Wind*, which had been caught out in
near gale force winds and rough seas. Late
at night the Skegness lifeboat and the Wells
lifeboat *Cecil Paine* both put out to search
for the vessel, which had been reported
overdue. At 5.30am on 20 April, *Charles
Fred Grantham* found the vessel aground
on the Frisney Flats so, when the tide
flooded, hauled her off the sands, took her
in tow, and brought her to Gibraltar Point.
On 5 June, the lifeboat went to another
pleasure craft, the cabin cruiser *Liz*, which
had a broken engine and was towed to
Grimsby. On 10 October, another pleasure
boat got into difficulty, the motor cruiser
Golden Spray, which had three people on

board. Its engine had broken down, so the
lifeboat towed the vessel to Boston.

The most difficult and arduous service
of the year was on 28 December when
Charles Fred Grantham assisted in the
search for survivors from the oil rig *Sea
Gem*. The rig had been converted from a
5,600-ton steel barge and was supported
on ten steel legs 50ft above the sea. Two
of these legs gave way as the craft was
being prepared to be moved to a new
location, and the whole rig tilted sideways
and sank. It sank about forty-seven miles
north-west of Cromer with heavy loss of
life. On board was a crew of thirty-seven,
of whom five died when the rig sank on
27 December, nineteen were saved by the
steamship *Baltrover*, which happened to be
passing, and eight men were missing.

Charles Fred Grantham was one of four
lifeboats involved in the search. The others
were from Wells, Cromer and the Humber,
and they spent a total of 113 hours at sea
searching for survivors. The Skegness
boat launched under Coxswain/Mechanic
Ken Holland at 6.30am and was at sea,
standing by the casualty and searching
for survivors for approximately fourteen
hours in severe weather, with extremely
difficult sea conditions, and intense cold.
She carried out a thorough search from
the north-east to the Dowsing lightvessel,

and then to the position of the casualty, returning past the Humber lightvessel and down the coast to Skegness. Despite the considerable efforts of all the rescue craft, no survivors were found.

The RNLI's Committee of Management recognised the efforts made by the Coxswains and crews of all the lifeboats involved, and praised the high standards of seamanship shown throughout the service. Additional monetary awards were made to each of the seven members of the Skegness crew, and Stirling Whorlow, the Institution's secretary, concluded: 'I should very much like to add to this letter an expression of my personal appreciation

of the manner in which the Coxswain and crew carried out the service.' A letter from BP, owners of the rig, was also received stating how much the company appreciated the crews' efforts.

The following year, 1966, the Skegness lifeboat was called out in more routine circumstances. On 23 March she landed an injured man and an RAF medical officer from the Lynn Well lightvessel, and on 21 May put out at 9.12pm in rough seas to go to the cabin cruiser *Higgy*, which had broken down three and a half miles east of Trusthorpe. A rubber dinghy was also reported missing, but nothing was found before the cruiser was reached.

The scene on the beach during the naming ceremony of Charles Fred Grantham, 9 July 1964. (By courtesy of RNLI Skegness)

Charles Fred Grantham on service to a US aircraft which had crashed in the Wisbech Channel, 5 August 1964. (By courtesy of Joel Grunnill)

Charles Fred Grantham launching on exercise some time in the late 1960s. The tractor T75, a Case 1000D type, was sent to the station in April 1964 at the same time as the new 37ft Oakely as she was more powerful than the previous launch vehicle. The pier, visible in the bottom photograph, was built in 1881 by the Earl of Scarbrough and was 1,000ft in length. It was wrecked in severe weather in January 1979. (By courtesy of Skegness RNLI)

Higgy was taken in tow and landed at Skegness by the inshore lifeboat, which had launched to help, enabling the lifeboat to resume the search for the dinghy. This was found at 7.30am the next day, and the survivors were taken to Skegness.

During 1969, similar services were undertaken. On 16 April, shortly before 4.30pm, *Charles Fred Grantham* was launched into choppy seas, and found the catamaran *Determination*, with four men on board, three miles south-east of Skegness. The vessel was towed to Gibraltar Point. On 29 August, *Charles Fred Grantham* and the inshore lifeboat were launched into rough seas to go to a dinghy which had fired a red flare. In rough seas, the lifeboat reached the dinghy which was a mile east of the pier at 2.40pm, and found her waterlogged with her engine broken.

The dinghy's two occupants were taken aboard the lifeboat, and the dinghy was hauled aboard. The survivors were landed at Skegness and both lifeboat and ILB were back at station within an hour of launching. The final service of the year came on 9 November after red flares had been seen fired from a speedboat with engine failure. *Charles Fred Grantham* was launched at 4.30pm into a north-westerly wind and found the speedboat. Its two crew were taken off by the lifeboat, which then towed the boat back to Skegness.

On three occasions during 1970 and 1971 the lifeboat was called upon to assist with medical evacuations. On 18 July 1970 and 12 June 1971, *Charles Fred Grantham* landed injured men from the Inner Dowsing lightvessel, and on 8 September 1971 she brought ashore the skipper of the steam tug *Northsider*, of Newcastle, who had had a heart attack. The lifeboat launched at 1.42am and within two hours returned to station where a doctor was waiting to attend to the skipper, who was taken to hospital.

On 2 November 1971, the lifeboat was involved in a long search when the German tanker *Waal*, of Duhort, radioed the coastguard after spotting a small sailing boat flying a distress signal eight and a half miles south-east of Skegness. The lifeboat launched at 1.33pm and the crew was told that the small vessel had drifted in a south-easterly direction. Two other vessels, the trawler *Young Elizabeth* and *Blatant*, had also heard the radio message and were already searching, so *Charles Fred Grantham* took the most easterly position. Visibility was poor, and a heavy sea was running, but, as the lifeboat crossed the Burnham Ridge, Signalman Morris Hatton spotted the missing vessel two miles away.

The boat was the 17ft clinker-built sloop-rigged dinghy *Black Rose* whose sails were torn. She was waterlogged, and the crew had been baling for eight hours. Coxswain Ken Holland took the

Charles Fred Grantham launching on service at 11pm on 19 April 1965 to the sloop Hal o' the Wind, which was overdue on passage. (Jeff Morris)

Charles Fred Grantham returning from service in rough seas on 20 April 1965 to the sloop Hal o' the Wind, which the lifeboat towed off the sands and brought safely to Gibraltar Point. (Jeff Morris)

Two photos showing Charles Fred Grantham returning to the boathouse after her service on 20 April 1965 to the sloop Hal o' the Wind. (Jeff Morris)

lifeboat alongside and Second Coxswain Joel Grunnill jumped aboard the sinking vessel and helped the crew get aboard the lifeboat. A tow line was attached, but *Black Rose* was so waterlogged that towing her was impossible and she eventually foundered seven miles north of the Lynn Well lightvessel. The lifeboat was beached at Skegness at 6.50pm and landed the dinghy's two occupants, who had left Boston the previous morning heading for Essex. They were full of praise for the lifeboatmen, with one saying: 'It was a marvellous sight to see the lifeboat coming. At first we would not believe it as we had seen one or two ships in the distance and none had spotted us and we thought that

this was another of them.'

During 1972, *Charles Fred Grantham* and her crew were fairly busy and saved no fewer than twenty lives. On the night of 17-18 February the lifeboat towed the Boston fishing vessel *Stremoy* and its two crew to the Boston river after the vessel had got into difficulty with a wire round its propeller. On 4 June both offshore and inshore lifeboats launched to the catamaran *Flying Witch*, which was dismasted and aground on Skegness Middle Sandbank. The ILB went alongside and managed to take off the five people on board, by when the lifeboat had arrived on scene. The survivors were transferred from the ILB to *Charles Fred Grantham*, and the ILB crew

Charles Fred Grantham tows the fishing boat Seeker into Boston on 25 June 1968. The lifeboat launched at 6.32am into rough seas to go to the vessel, which was aground on the Butterwick Low Sands. The Boston pilot boat Elsie Wing was standing by, and an RAF helicopter winched up one man and landed him ashore. At 8.30am the lifeboat took the boat in tow, and the vessel was taken to Boston harbour. (By courtesy of Joel Grunnill)

went back to the casualty to try to save it. However, they were unable to get it off the sands, and had to leave the vessel which subsequently broke up. On 22 August the injured skipper of the German coaster *Adda*, of Hamburg, eleven miles from Skegness, was brought ashore to be taken to hospital after sustaining a shoulder injury. The station's medical officer, Dr Alex Jamieson, went out with the lifeboat to treat the injured man. Three days later the skipper was put back onto his vessel with the coaster's agents defraying all expenses incurred by the lifeboat.

The most dramatic rescue of the year occurred on 2 December, when the lifeboat was launched into heavy seas and high winds to search for the 38ft fishing vessel *Silver Surf*. Coxswain Holland took the lifeboat through the Wainfleet Swatchway to the Boston Deeps, where it was thought *Silver Surf* might be found. The lifeboat crew, as they peered through the driving spray, spotted the vessel's mast on the opposite side of the Long Sand.

After cutting through the Parlour Channel in dangerously heavy seas, the lifeboat reached the Lynn Deeps and went alongside the heaving and rolling casualty. A towline was passed and *Silver Surf*, with a crew of two, was towed up the river Welland to Fosdyke. The vessel's nets had fouled its propeller, and its anchors would not hold. In fact both anchors had been lost by the time the lifeboat arrived,

reaching *Silver Surf* just in time to prevent her breaking up on the sands. 'This launch was a severe test for *Charles Fred Grantham*, and she handled admirably in the conditions,' said Coxswain Holland.

On 3 December 1972, the relief lifeboat *Calouste Gulbenkian* came to the station, and stayed until 5 August 1973. Of the two launches she undertook during her nine-month stint at Skegness, only one resulted in an effective service. This came on 9 July 1973, when she went to the fishing boat *Flying Cloud*, which was fishing for mussels in the Boston Deeps off Wrangle Flats. The fishing boat capsized in heavy seas, but the owner managed to swim ashore to raise the alarm. The lifeboat launched at 5.20am in light winds and smooth seas to search for the other man from the fishing vessel. The capsized fishing boat was found at 7am and an unsuccessful attempt was made to right the vessel. The lifeboat then proceeded to search for the missing man as the crew realised he was not underneath the vessel. At 9.46am a helicopter reported a body in the water and so the ILB, which was assisting in the search, picked it up and transferred it on board *Calouste Gulbenkian* to be landed ashore.

In 1975, the lifeboat station celebrated its 150th anniversary. To commemorate the event a special anniversary launch took place on Saturday 16 August, when the Vice-Chairman of the RNLI, Lieut

Cdr P. E. C. Pickles, RNVR, presented the station with a framed vellum. The lifeboat, dressed overall, was drawn up on Tower Esplanade. Cdr Pickles inspected members of the crew and launchers, past and present, who were lined up alongside the lifeboat. At the end of the ceremony, District Inspector M. G. K. Fennel presented Honorary Secretary Neville Ball with a pair of binoculars in recognition of his ten years' service in the post.

During summer 1975 both lifeboats undertook several launches, with the offshore lifeboat's first service coming on 28 June when she spent more than two hours at sea saving the yacht *Marza*, in difficulty a mile off the beach, and its only occupant. On 16 July, sixteen people were rescued from one of the DUKW pleasure craft used on the beach after the craft began drifting a mile north of the pier after its engine had broken down. On 24 November the crew of an RAF Phantom aircraft from Coningsby, who baled out over the pier after their aircraft had a hydraulic failure, were picked up by *Charles Fred Grantham*.

The lifeboat launched at 2.18pm and quickly reached the airmen, picking them up a few minutes before a helicopter from RAF Coltishall arrived. The pilot, Flight Lieut Mike Smith, and navigator, Flight Lieut Rob Lunn, were both uninjured and returned to their base none the worse for their experience. Honorary Secretary Neville Ball was full of praise for the lifeboat crew, commenting: 'It was about the fastest launch I have ever seen'. The

Shield presented to the lifeboat crew by the RAF after the service to the crashed Phantom aircraft in November 1975. The shield is mounted on a wooden frame and displayed in the lifeboat house . (Nicholas Leach)

Charles Fred Grantham towing in a fishing boat to Gibraltar Point. (By courtesy of Joel Grunnill)

crew and launchers were entertained at RAF Coningsby the following week in thanks for the rescue, and a letter of appreciation signed by the RNLI's Chief of Operations was sent to the station.

The first service of 1977 took place on 13 January, only two hours before the lifeboat was due to be launched on a routine exercise. The 60ft fishing vessel *Thor* (GY105), of Boston, requested assistance after a net had fouled her propeller. *Thor* reported her position as half a mile due east of the Lynn Knock Buoy, but drifted on the ebb tide two miles north-east of this position. As soon as the alarm was raised at 3pm, *Charles Fred Grantham* was launched and kept in radio contact with the fishing vessel, which was about seven miles from Skegness.

The lifeboat reached the casualty to find conditions on scene appalling. The crew were faced with a force nine easterly gale, intense cold, and heavy seas with snow and sleet blizzards reducing visibility to

Skegness lifeboat crew, 1977. From left to right: Coxswain Ken Holland, Second Coxswain Joel Grunnill, Bowman Ron Chapman, Assistant Mechanic Johnny Strzelecki, Maurice Hatton, Colin Moore, Graham Phillips and Honorary Secretary Neville Ball. (By courtesy of Joel Grunnill)

only a few yards. Towing the casualty to Gibraltar Point was impossible with the weather deteriorating further. So, it was decided to bring the boat to Skegness, anchor her in deep water, and take off the two crew. However, soon after the lifeboat took *Thor* in tow, the seas increased and the tow line snapped. It was reconnected, only to snap again when off Skegness. Visibility had become so bad by this time that the lifeboat crew were unsure of their position, although they knew they were in the vicinity of Skegness pier.

Heavy seas continued to break over both vessels, and the fishing boat was proving too heavy for the lifeboat to hold. As both vessels were driven ashore in the surf, the fishermen were taken on board the lifeboat to safety in an operation that damaged the lifeboat. She came ashore opposite Tower Esplanade and the shore crew then began to recover *Charles Fred Grantham*, a difficult task undertaken in some of the most hostile conditions encountered on the beach for over thirty years. Thick ice formed on the hull of the lifeboat, only dropping off as the boat was hauled ashore. The blizzard increased to such an extent that the sleet and snow made it almost impossible for the launchers to see what they were doing.

Several launchers went out on the tractor to connect the warp to the lifeboat, all wearing lifejackets, and were swept by the breaking seas. But eventually, the tractor reached the lifeboat and brought her into shallower water, the skids were laid and the lifeboat was dragged up the beach. The launchers were at times up to their waists in icy water, but carried on regardless until the recovery was completed. *Charles Fred Grantham* was then housed, while both survivors were landed unhurt, apart from suffering severely from the cold.

The other services during 1977 were somewhat less testing. On 16 May, she saved the yacht *Danora* and her three crew, in difficulty four miles from Skegness, and on 9 July went to the 23ft yacht *Springtime*, whose two crew were exhausted and seasick, nine miles north-east of the pier. On reaching *Springtime*, the lifeboat transferred a lifeboatman aboard who helped sail the vessel back to Wainfleet Haven with the lifeboat

escorting, returning to station after almost ten hours at sea. On 6 September she launched at 7.08am to the twin-engined motor boat *Jasmina*, which was on passage from the Humber to Great Yarmouth but became disabled ten miles east of Skegness. The boat was also towed to Wainfleet Haven from Scott Patch.

In September 1977, *Charles Fred Grantham* went for refit, leaving station on 26 September and calling at Wells on her way to Lowestoft where her crew picked up relief lifeboat *Calouste Gulbenkian*, which stood in for the station boat. *Charles Fred Grantham* arrived at Fletcher's Yard at Oulton Broad, Lowestoft, on 3 October and was surveyed and overhauled. She was also fitted with radar, becoming the fifth Oakley lifeboat to receive such equipment.

During six months at Skegness, *Calouste Gulbenkian* launched four times on service, although her most difficult launch was not included in these figures as it ended without an effective service. She launched at 4.40pm on 11 January 1978 in a very rough sea and force ten northerly storm force winds to go to the assistance of the Greek ship *Gloriosa*, which was in

difficulties in the Wash. The ship was manoeuvring with difficulty in the heavy seas and strong winds while attempting to reach the King's Lynn approaches. The lifeboat made good progress in a heavy following sea, but was recalled before she got to the casualty as it reached shelter unaided. After battling back to Skegness against a wind that was now gusting to force twelve and worsening heavy seas, Coxswain Ken Holland decided to wait offshore until the extremely heavy surf moderated as conditions on the beach were very dangerous.

While waiting offshore, with the drogue streamed, a radio message was received stating that red flares had been reported off the Norfolk coast, thirty miles to the east, and neither Cromer nor Wells lifeboats could get away because of difficulties in the crews reaching their respective stations. In the horrendous conditions, with the prospect of a five-hour passage just to reach the scene, and having already been at sea for four hours, the lifeboat crew agreed to proceed only if the reports of the sighting proved to be definite. As only one unconfirmed

Charles Fred Grantham beaching ready for recovery. This shows the boat before the radar or enclosed cockpit were fitted. (By courtesy of Skegness RNLI)

Coxswain/Mechanic Kenneth Holland on board the lifeboat. He joined the lifeboat crew in 1946, became bowman in 1947, Coxswain in 1965 and Coxswain/Mechanic from 1969. He was elected Mayor of Skegness in 1981 and is pictured here with his mayoral chain. (By courtesy of the RNLI)

sighting had been reported, a response could not be justified in the conditions, so the lifeboat was prepared for recovery. However, before returning to the beach at 10.40pm, six hours after launching, *Charles Fred Grantham* had to be taken further offshore to avoid floating and flying debris from the pier, much of which had been destroyed by the exceptionally high tide and heavy seas.

On 1 May 1978, *Charles Fred Grantham* returned to Skegness, having been overhauled and fitted with a Decca 060 radar set. Her first service after her return took place on 5 July, when she assisted a yacht whose crew were unsure of their position, three miles off Skegness. On 4 October 1978 she went to the King's Lynn

Paul Martin, Coxswain/Mechanic from July 1985 to May 1989 and from January 1990 to December 1999. He originally joined the crew as beach launcher and ILB crew in 1968. He spent nine months as Second Coxswain until being appointed Coxswain/Mechanic in 1985. (By courtesy of the RNLI)

vessel *Fair Maid*, a 55ft beam trawler, which was in difficulty off Ingoldmells. The vessel was disabled and taking in water, with only the skipper aboard. Several lifeboat crew were transferred aboard to assist baling, and the lifeboat towed the vessel to Wainfleet Haven. Because of the risk of the vessel sinking and blocking the river, *Fair Maid* was anchored in shallow water on the south bar just inside the river mouth so that her hull could be inspected at low water. The skipper was taken off and the lifeboat returned to station.

During 1979, *Charles Fred Grantham* performed some unusual services, starting on 10 July when she launched at 1pm to help an injured seaman on board the German ship *Rubin*, which was anchored to the east of the Freeman Channel. Dr G. Morris, the station's Honorary Medical Advisor, and a lifeboatman were put aboard the ship. The doctor examined the seaman but decided not to attempt to evacuate the injured man, who had a damaged back, and instead stayed aboard while the ship proceeded to Boston Dock. Once the vessel was in port, the casualty was taken to hospital by ambulance.

Her next service, on 14 August 1979, came after a night of severe gales when two yachts were seen anchored close in. In a heavy sea and a south-south-westerly force nine gale, *Charles Fred Grantham* was launched following worries about the yachts' safety. The first one, *Xanthe*, with her sails blown out, was escorted as far as Mablethorpe on her way to the shelter of the Humber. The second, *Mavis M*, could not recover her anchor, even with the help of two lifeboatmen who were put aboard with great difficulty in the conditions. The lifeboatmen and the yacht's two crew were taken off and the lifeboat returned to the beach leaving the craft at anchor. During the night, the strong winds continued unabated, and the next day the yacht was found twenty-two miles east of Skegness after the anchor chain snapped.

In 1981, the lifeboat went to cargo vessels on two separate occasions. On 19 February 1981, while Divisional Inspector Tom Nutman was aboard to check the boat and crew, *Charles Fred Grantham* was diverted to the coaster *Drie Breeders*, which was listing and had lost engine

Relief 37ft Oakley lifeboat Calouste Gulbenkian on the beach in 1977. She stood in on relief duty at Skegness three times: in 1972–73, 1977–78 and 1983–84. The crew with her are, left to right, Paul Martin, Morris Hatton, John Strzelecki, Ron Chapman, Joel Grunnill and Coxswain Ken Holland. (By courtesy of Joel Grunnill)

power in rough seas fifteen miles east of Skegness. By the time the lifeboat arrived, the coaster's crew had restored limited power but, as the vessel was still listing, the lifeboat escorted it through heavy seas to the shelter of the Wash.

The next month, on 14 March, *Charles Fred Grantham* launched at 5.35pm and spent twenty-two hours on service to the Limassol-registered coaster *Amsel*, which was sinking ten miles south-south-east of Skegness. Three of the coaster's crew were taken off by a Sea King helicopter from RAF Coltishall, leaving three still aboard to try to save the ship, with the lifeboat standing by. After failing to negotiate an acceptable deal with the ocean-going tug *Salvageman*, *Amsel's* master decided that the only way to save his ship was to run her onto the Sunk Sand on the falling tide. The lifeboat's emergency mechanic was put aboard to help, and *Amsel* was then run up the sandbank, while the lifeboat stood by. The lifeboat eventually returned to Skegness at 3.30pm the following day.

Another long service launch took place on 28 February 1982, when *Charles Fred Grantham* was at sea for fifteen hours after launching to search for a man missing in the speedboat *Lightening* off Mablethorpe in poor visibility and choppy seas. The Skegness and Humber lifeboats searched throughout the night, with other vessels and a helicopter also joining the search,

coordinated by the Humber lifeboat. The casualty was spotted by the Humber lifeboat crew the following day, ten miles out from the Humber, and was rescued and landed at Grimsby. A letter of appreciation signed by the RNLI's Chief of Operations, Cdr D. B. Cairns RNR, was sent to Coxswain Ken Holland and the crew in recognition of their efforts during this service in which they were searching for more than fifteen hours.

Later that year, on 19 December 1982, the lifeboat was at sea for five hours in south-south-westerly storm force ten winds and heavy seas escorting the cargo vessel *Cedra Sun*, which was carrying a deck cargo of timber. The vessel was eleven miles east-north-east of Skegness, near the Inner Dowsing light tower, and had developed a severe list to starboard after her cargo shifted. She was making very slow progress in heavy seas. However, when the lifeboat reached the casualty and went alongside, the vessel's skipper preferred not to leave, but stay aboard and try to save his ship. So the lifeboat escorted the vessel south, to the safety of the King's Lynn approaches. Some of the timber that was washed overboard subsequently ended up on beaches in and around Skegness.

The only service performed by *Charles Fred Grantham* during 1983 took place on 14 January after a southerly gale caught out some of the Boston fishing fleet.

Two of the fleet, *Provider* and *Angelina*, while on passage back from fishing in the Thames estuary, were reported overdue so the lifeboat launched at 7.20am. The vessels were found twelve miles south of Skegness entering the Wash, with *Angelina* being towed by the cargo vessel *Nautic W* ending up in Wells. The lifeboat escorted the vessels to the Boston approaches and stood by two other fishing vessels, *Onward*

and *Frederick J*, until they safely reached harbour. The lifeboat ended up having to go to Wells, and then returned to Skegness for recovery having been out for almost ten hours.

In the early afternoon of 24 July 1984, an aircraft crashed into the sea somewhere east of Skegness and the ILB was launched immediately. After proceeding a short distance, the craft was recalled by

Skegness lifeboat crew with Charles Fred Grantham, from left to right, Philip Lill (Chairman), Neville Ball (Honorary Secretary), Dale Chapman, Ray Chapman, Terry Wallace, Fraser Disney, Brian Wright, Graham Phillips, John Goulton, Ron Chapman, John Griffiths, John Strzelecki, Brian Porter, Morris Hatton, Joel Grunnill, Colin Moore and Ken Holland (Coxswain). (By courtesy of Joel Grunnill)

Charles Fred Grantham at sea off the beach after she had been fitted with radar. (From an old postcard supplied by Joel Grunnill)

the Coastguard, who had received reports from the Norfolk coast and dispatched Hunstanton inshore lifeboat to the Brancaster area. After further consultation, the ILB was relaunched, followed at 1.30pm by *Charles Fred Grantham*. Both lifeboats headed out at full speed in the direction of the first sighting.

The ILB crew soon spotted orange smoke flares, which had been set off by three survivors who were clinging to flotation bags, below which hung their submerged helicopter. The men were taken aboard the ILB and later transferred to RAF rescue helicopter 125, which flew them directly to hospital. Coxswain Ken Holland decided to try to save the aircraft, so, with the assistance of the ILB and the Hunstanton Atlantic 21 inshore lifeboat, a line was attached and the long tow back to Skegness commenced. On arrival, the aircraft was carefully dragged up the beach to be examined and later removed.

On 26 September 1985, *Charles Fred Grantham* was launched on what proved to be a testing service which lasted fourteen hours. She put out at 7.40am to the angling vessel *Challenge*, with twenty-two persons on board, which had not returned to her home port of Grimsby after a fishing trip off the Humber. The lifeboat was tasked to search for the vessel, with the Humber and Bridlington lifeboats also involved, as well as a Nimrod aircraft and two SAR helicopters. The casualty was eventually located off Mablethorpe and its crew was taken off by the D class inflatable, with both Humber and Skegness lifeboats arriving shortly afterwards. *Charles Fred Grantham*, because she had

a shallower draught than the Humber lifeboat, towed the fishing boat into deeper water, and then handed it over to the Humber lifeboat. However, the Humber boat was called away to assist two cobles in difficulties north of the Humber, so the Skegness lifeboat resumed and completed the tow to the Humber.

Another arduous service was undertaken on 5 April 1986 when *Charles Fred Grantham* launched at 12.30pm into very heavy seas with a north-easterly force six wind to go to the assistance of the yacht *Sterentjie*, which was in trouble seven miles north of Skegness. The yacht was taking a pounding in the heavy surf, but the crew managed to reach the shore. The yacht had problems with its rudder and, as the skipper was intending to attempt to refloat

Relief lifeboat Calouste Gulbenkian off Skegness beach, 21 July 1984. She stood in from 25 July 1983 to 22 July 1984, but did not complete any effective services during that time. (By courtesy of Skegness RNLI)

Charkles Fred Grantham after her refit at J. E. Fletcher's boatyard, 17 July 1984. She had a new fully enclosed cockpit shelter fitted, providing much better protection for her crew. (By courtesy of Skegness RNLI)

Two photos showing the relief 37ft Oakley Calouste Gulbenkian being taken along the tower esplanade and across the central beach by Case 1150B tractor T89 in 1984. This tractor served the station from July 1979 to October 1984. (By courtesy of Trevor Holland)

October 1984 marked an end of an era at Skegness lifeboat station with the retirement of Joel Grunnill leaving no member of the Grunnill family serving as crew. Joel had been on the crew from 1939 to 1951, when he became Second Coxswain, a position he held until retirement in 1984. He later became a Deputy Launching Authority and subsequently Honorary Secretary. (By courtesy of Skegness RNLI)

her, the lifeboat was asked to stand by. With a heavy surf running, breakwaters either side and a strong flood tide, the yacht was in significant danger.

The lifeboat was anchored outside the surf and then veered down into the breakers to within 100m of the yacht in very shallow water. A rocket line was fired ashore to pass a long tow rope to the yacht, which was bow to sea, and her stern was tied to a tractor. The lifeboat tightened up on the anchor cable and the tow rope, so that when the line holding her to the tractor was cut, the yacht was catapulted through the surf by the stretched nylon tow rope and the lifeboat motoring to seawards. The anchor was recovered and the yacht was towed to the safety of the Wainfleet Haven.

In September 1986, *Charles Fred Grantham* was taken to Whisstock's yard at Woodbridge, Suffolk, for a survey and hull repairs. She was more than twenty years old, and concern had been expressed about possible deterioration of her hull timbers. The water ballast tank that gave the 37ft Oakley its stability in the water and provided the self-righting capability, proved somewhat problematic in the long term. The aluminium alloy construction of the inner bottom, which on entry into the water was filled with salt water, acted like a huge battery and caused the planking of the hull to deteriorate over time through the process of electrolysis. As a result, during the mid-1980s several of the Oakleys in service suffered serious hull deterioration, and many had to be virtually rebuilt. The hull of *Charles Fred Grantham* was completely replanked before the boat returned to station in 1988.

In place of the station boat came the relief Oakley *Mary Joicey*, stationed at Newbiggin until April 1981 before entering the Relief Fleet. She was brought to Skegness on 6 October 1986 and stayed at the station for more than a year. By the time she departed on 28 March 1988, she had launched seven times on service.

Her longest service took place on 10 February 1987 when she put out at 4.50am in near gale force winds to go to the King's Lynn fishing vessel *Lady Joan*, which had a fouled propeller in heavy seas eleven miles south-west of Skegness. The vessel had been anchored off the Sunk Sand the previous night, and two other trawlers had come to assist but were unable to get close enough to pass a line, so requested lifeboat assistance.

By the time the lifeboat reached *Lady Joan*, the vessel's anchor chain had parted, and she was being pushed rapidly up the edge of the Sunk Sand by a strong ebb tide and gale force winds. The lifeboat reached her at dawn and, after several attempts, a heavy tow was passed despite the fishing vessel rolling and plunging heavily in the bad conditions. The full length of tow rope, with a tyre in the middle as a shock absorber, was deployed by the lifeboat crew, and then the tow began towards the shelter of the Lynn approaches. Here, she was handed over to another fishing vessel and the lifeboat returned to station after ten hours at sea.

Charles Fred Grantham returned to station on 27 March 1988 and completed a number of services during 1988. The longest took place on 25 June 1988 after the vessel *Ben Lora*, on passage from

Spain to Grimsby with four crew, went aground in the entrance to the Humber. The description of the surroundings led Coxswain Paul Martin to believe the vessel's position to be the Dogsheads in the Wash rather than in the Humber. So, after contacting the Coastguard, he readied the lifeboat and she launched at 4.30pm into calm seas and light winds. She soon found the casualty, whose crew had mistaken Gibraltar Point for Spurn Head, hard aground on the west side of the Inner Dogs Head. The lifeboat stayed alongside until the next high water when she pulled

Relief 37ft Oakley Mary Joicey arriving at Skegness on 6 October 1986. She was brought to the station from Blyth, having had an eight-month refit at Amble, by Coxswain Paul Martin, Second Coxswain Ron Chapman, Assistant Mechanic Graham Phillips, and crew members Maurice Hatton and Brian Wright. They sailed to Whitby for an overnight stop, before undertaking the eleven-hour passage to Skegness. (By courtesy of Ben Hardaker)

the vessel off and guided her through the sandbanks to deeper water to continue her passage to the Humber. The lifeboat then returned to station, having been at sea for about twelve hours.

Another long service was undertaken on 29 May 1989 when *Charles Fred Grantham* went to the fishing vessel *Barry Williams* (LN 135), which was on passage from the Humber to the Thames estuary. At 5.37pm, her skipper called for immediate assistance as the vessel was taking water through and only expected to stay afloat for another thirty minutes. A Wessex helicopter carrying a pump

was scrambled from RAF Coltishall and *Charles Fred Grantham* was launched, although the fifteen-mile passage to the casualty would take about two hours. The helicopter reached *Barry Williams* before the vessel sank and, having pumped her out, the crew were able to make temporary repairs to prevent further ingress of water. The lifeboat reached the scene, and took the casualty in tow to Boston, reaching port at 2am on 30 May.

Charles Fred Grantham was involved in a widespread search centred over the bombing ranges of the Wash on 5 February 1990 after an aircraft crashed four miles south of the Wainfleet Range. The lifeboat was launched and, in the dark, proceeded down to the Boston Deeps, making good use of the recently fitted Furuno radar. The Boston pilot vessel and Hunstanton Atlantic 21 inshore lifeboat found some wreckage and later a body, while the Skegness lifeboat searched further down tide, picking up further wreckage. Several aircraft were also involved, and Coastguard Auxiliary teams worked the shoreline together with USAF personnel, but neither of the two crew from the American F-111 aircraft survived the crash and resulting explosion when it hit the water over the marsh. The Skegness lifeboat continued searching, using parachute flares and searchlights, but only

found more wreckage, and the search was called off in the early hours.

What proved to be the last effective service of *Charles Fred Grantham* took place on 15 April 1990 when she launched at 7.15pm to the motor cruiser *Lady Rysal*, in difficulty ten miles off Skegness, and towed the craft to safety. Before the end of July 1990, the lifeboat twice to investigate reports of red flares, and the other launch resulted in a night-time search for the yacht *Windquest 2*, reported overdue in the Round Lincolnshire Race, but this proved to be a false alarm.

Charles Fred Grantham left Skegness on 9 August 1988 and was taken to Leggett's boatyard at Grimsby, and was reallocated to the Relief Fleet. Between arriving at Skegness in April 1964 and being replaced in August 1990, she was credited with 148 service launches and saving ninety-six lives. From October 1990 to April 1991 she served on relief at Scarborough and Filey after which she was taken by road to Branksea Marine at Wareham, Dorset. She stayed here in storage for almost two years until, in March 1993, she was broken up.

Inshore lifeboats 1973-90

While the offshore lifeboat launched on services usually in challenging conditions, the station's inshore lifeboat gave an

The first tractor used to launch the ILB was a Massey Ferguson 135, pictured in 1984 outside the small ILB house. This vehicle, on the station from 1983 until the late 1990s, was bought by money was raised locally at a cost of cost £480. The house, just seaward of the present lifeboat station, was used from the late 1960s until 1990. (Trevor Holland)

important rapid response to rescues closer to shore, and undertook an increasing number of services throughout the 1970s and 1980s. In March 1973 a new ILB, D-212, was sent to the station and served until 1987 making her the longest-serving ILB. During that time she is credited with saving eighty-three lives in 281 launches.

Amongst the more unusual services performed was one on 5 May 1977 after a longhorn steer escaped from the abattoir. The beast ran through the town causing panic amongst the public in the main street as it headed to the beach where it started swimming out to sea. The ILB launched and, having lassoed the creature, the crew tied it alongside their craft and brought it back to the beach. Here, much to the crew's dislike, it was somewhat

unnecessarily killed by a slaughterman.

Typical of services performed by the inshore lifeboats were those to small pleasure craft, bathers, and children on airbeds being blown out to sea. In 1982, of fourteen lives saved by the ILB, thirteen were from airbeds. On 22 August 1985 a ten-year-old girl had a lucky escape when she was blown out to sea off Ingoldmells by a force five westerly wind. Her parents unsuccessfully tried to swim to her, but were forced to return to the beach. By the time the ILB had reached the scene, the inflatable had capsized and a lifeguard from the beach had swum out and was trying to keep the girl above water, about 400 yards offshore. The ILB took both the girl and the lifeguard on board and returned them to the beach. The girl was suffering from shock and exposure, and was thoroughly exhausted by her ordeal.

On 27 October 1985, two men working on the pier head were taken off by the ILB after the tide came in and, with the walk-way to the shore unusable, trapped them. They had not been able to put out a smouldering fire and feared that the whole structure was in danger of burning. These fears were confirmed as, later that night, the structure was completely gutted, leaving just a tangle of twisted metal. This was the end for the pier, which was built in 1881 but had to be demolished.

In January 1987, a new inshore lifeboat, D-326, was sent to the station. Funded by the Wolvers family of Lincoln, she

Naming and dedication ceremony of the new inshore lifeboat D-326 Michel Philippe Wolvers on 9 August 1987 at a ceremony held in the Peace Gardens, Tower Esplanade. The service of dedication was conducted by the Rev Ernest Adley, Rector of Skegness Church of England. The three crew by the boat are, left to right, Richard Foye, Ian Johnson and Senior Helmsman Ray Chapman. (By courtesy of Skegness RNLI)

was named *Michel Philippe Wolvers*, in memory of the family member who, on 6 July 1984, was lost overboard from a merchant ship on which he was Third Officer. The new lifeboat was handed over during a ceremony on 9 August 1987 with Philip Lill, chairman of the station, presiding. Ian Wolvers, donor of the lifeboat, handed the boat into the care of the RNLI and she was accepted by Ray Kipling, the Institution's assistant director. He handed the craft into the care of the station and she was accepted by Honorary Secretary Terry Smart. At the end of the ceremony, the new ILB was launched and demonstrated to the assembled crowd.

Before her official naming, the new ILB had performed five services, two in June and three in July. Her first rescue came on 1 June 1987, when she went out ten miles to help a broken-down fishing vessel. The

The inshore lifeboat crew in 1989 were from left to right, front to back, Ray Chapman, Ian Johnson, Richard Watson, Mick Clark, Terry Smart, Tim Champness, Ray McDermot, Brian Porter, Mick Abbott, Paul Maltby, Richard Foye and Andy Epton; sitting in the boat is John Irving. (By courtesy of Skegness RNLI)

In front of a large crowd of holiday-makers and locals, Charles Fred Grantham being launched on 31 July 1990 to welcome home her successor, Lincolnshire Poacher. (Jeff Morris)

D class inflatable D-326 Michel Philippe Wolvers inside the ILB house. The crew with her are, from left to right, Ray Chapman, unknown, Ian Johnson, Andy Wright, Brian Porter, unknown, Mick Clark, Paul Maltby, unknown, Joel Grunnill, Alan Sewell, John Irving, Mick Abbott (on boat), Ray McDermott. Standing on the left are Richard Watson, Andy Epton and Carl Francis. (By courtesy of Skegness RNLI)

next three launches all turned out to be false alarms, but on 31 July 1987, the ILB was launched very rapidly to an inflatable dinghy five miles north-east of the town. The ILB crew found two boys, aged eleven and sixteen, in the water hanging on to the craft and being blown out to sea. Both were suffering from exposure and in need of hospital treatment, so were quickly brought ashore. During 1987 the D class boathouse was extended to provide improved crew facilities.

After a series of routine services in 1988, the following year proved to be particularly busy for the ILB with *Michel Philippe Wolvers* launching twenty-two times on service, often with no outcome. The first service, on 19 April 1989, involved both lifeboats as they often work together to cover a search area more rapidly, or the ILB will request the offshore lifeboat for support should the weather deteriorate or the helmsman consider further assistance is required. The ILB put out at 3pm to the fishing vessel *Maria Carmen*, which was taking on water three and a half miles north-north-east of Skegness. *Charles Fred Grantham*

was launched as backup and, when the fishermen stemmed the leak on their boat, both lifeboats escorted the casualty ashore.

The ILB had another busy day on 27 July 1989 after three young girls were blown out to sea off the central beach. The ILB launched at 3.27pm and soon reached the three girls and two exhausted lifeguards hanging onto a canoe, which was helping to keep them all afloat. The ILB brought the five ashore, with the three girls needing hospital treatment. The boat had already launched that morning, putting out to an abandoned rubber dinghy. Most of the calls on the ILB came from pleasure craft, with sailboards, sailing dinghies and power boats often getting into trouble.

During 1989, the ILB went out on two separate occasions to the same speedboat, *Disco Diner*. First, at 5.54pm on 24 July the ILB launched and towed the vessel and its three occupants to shore after it had broken down four miles from Skegness. On 24 August, the ILB again went to the speedboat, which this time had seven persons on board, but had broken down in an almost identical location.

Lincolnshire Poacher

In July 1990 a new lifeboat, *Lincolnshire Poacher*, arrived at Skegness. A Mersey class, she was completely different from any previous boat to serve the station. The type was designed and developed by the RNLI during the 1980s for stations where the lifeboat was carriage launched, to replace the 37ft Oakleys which were at the end of their operational lives. The new design, a major technological advance over the Oakley, was self-righting by virtue of the inherent buoyancy of the watertight wheelhouse, which also contained seating for six crew, an additional seat for a doctor, as well as the latest navigation and communication equipment.

The most notable difference between the old and the new boats was the speed; powered by twin 285hp Caterpillar 3208T turbo-charged diesels, the Mersey was capable of more than seventeen knots, about twice that of the Oakley. This power also gave her much greater manoeuvrability. Approximately 245 gallons of fuel were carried giving a range, at full speed, of 145 nautical miles. The lifeboat could be controlled from within the wheelhouse, or from a flying bridge for work at close-quarters. To enable the boat to be launched from a carriage, the propellers were protected by the hull form, which incorporated a tunnel stern and extended bilge keels that supported the weight of the boat on the beach, protecting the propellers and rudders from being damaged during the recovery procedure.

The first eight boats of the class were constructed from aluminium, while later boats were made from fibre-reinforced composite (FRC). The Skegness boat was the seventh of the eight aluminium craft to be built. The hull was built by Aluminium Shipbuilders at Portsmouth, and then towed over to the Isle of Wight to be fitted out at Souter Shipyard, Cowes, at a total cost of £460,212. She successfully passed her self-righting trials at Cowes during the spring of 1990 and in early July 1990 Coxswain/Mechanic Paul Martin, Second Coxswain John Irving and Assistant Mechanic Graham Philips attended five days of boat and engine trials with passages from Cowes to Alderney and as

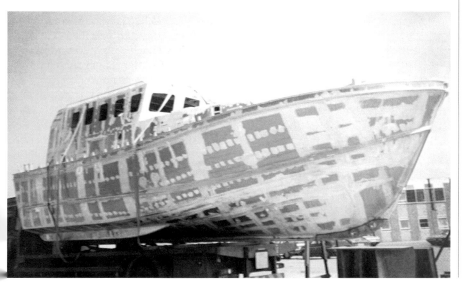

The aluminium hull of the new 12m Mersey allocated to Skegness ready to be fitted out at Souter Shipyard, Cowes. (By courtesy of Skegness RNLI)

far west as Falmouth, before returning to the RNLI Depot at Poole.

To fund the new lifeboat a special appeal was launched, the Lincolnshire Lifeboat Appeal, at RAF Swinderby in March 1989 with the intention of raising £600,000 to fund the new boat and boathouse. The Appeal's working group was chaired by Jack Roughton CBE, with Colonel Eric Foster as secretary, and hoped to raise the total amount from within Lincolnshire. The target was reached before the boat was delivered and, as all the funds were raised in the county including a considerable donation from the John and Lucille Van Geest Charitable Trust of Spalding, it was decided that the lifeboat would be named *Lincolnshire Poacher*.

New lifeboat house

To accommodate the new lifeboat, a new boathouse was built on Tower Esplanade, much closer to the sea than the 1893 house. Work began in 1989 on the new building which, completed in July 1990 at a cost of just over £160,000, was the first boathouse purpose-built for a Mersey and the first new lifeboat house built by the RNLI for an all-weather lifeboat for more than two decades. The boathouse was large enough to take both the new Mersey and inshore lifeboats, with their associated launch vehicles, and provided much better crew facilities than the old house as well as a souvenir outlet. In 1998, a new lookout was built adjoining the boathouse, on the beach side, providing improved crew accommodation as well as new changing facilities for the ILB crew.

Between 23 and 27 July 1990 Coxswain/ Mechanic Paul Martin and six crew attended a special familiarisation course at the RNLI Headquarters in Poole during which they trained on board the new Mersey class lifeboat. The lifeboatmen carried out various practical exercises as well as studying the lifeboat's capabilities in classroom work in the Training Centre in Poole. Practical exercises included communications, radar and navigation and the use of all equipment. Emergency procedures, such as man overboard drill, fire-fighting, engine and steering failure were practised, together with a winching drill involving an SAR helicopter.

On completion of the course, the crew sailed for Skegness with Tom Nutman, Divisional Inspector for the Eastern Division, in command, in the early hours of 28 July. The lifeboat reached Skegness on 31 July, having called at Newhaven, Ramsgate overnight, Lowestoft and Boston overnight en route north. A large crowd greeted the boat with both *Charles Fred Grantham* and the ILB launching to welcome her to the station. A week of intensive launch and recovery trials followed so that any problems with the launch procedure could be resolved, and the new boat was officially placed on station on 7 August 1990. *Charles Fred Grantham* then launched from Skegness for the last time and headed to Grimsby from where, after a brief paint up, she joined the Relief Fleet.

Arrival of the new 12m Mersey Lincolnshire Poacher on 31 July 1990, escorted home by 37ft Oakley Charles Fred Grantham. The top photo shows the new boat passing the beach for the benefit of the crowds gathered to welcome her home. (Jeff Morris)

Charles Fred Grantham is recovered after welcoming home the new 12m Mersey lifeboat in July 1990. (Jeff Morris)

The new lifeboat was formally named *Lincolnshire Poacher* at a ceremony on Sunday 30 September 1990, at which the new lifeboat house was also opened. The rather wet weather accompanying the event did not dampen the enthusiasm of the large crowd which gathered outside the new boathouse. Basil Major, Chairman of the Branch, opened proceedings and Jack Roughton, Chairman of the Lincolnshire Lifeboat Appeal, invited Michael Vernon, Chairman of the RNLI, to formally open the lifeboat house. The lifeboat was formally handed over to the RNLI by Mrs Lucille Van Geest, who had made a large donation to the appeal.

The boat was accepted by Mr Vernon who then passed her to Honorary Secretary Terry Smart and into the care of the Skegness station. The service of dedication was conducted by the Rev Stuart Ripley, Rural Dean, assisted by the

Lincolnshire Poacher is recovered for the first time following her arrival on 31 July 1990, watched by a large crowd. (Jeff Morris)

Lincolnshire Poacher is recovered for the first time following her arrival, 31 July 1990. (Jeff Morris)

Lincolnshire Poacher is recovered onto her carriage for the first time following her arrival, 31 July 1990. (Jeff Morris)

First launch from Skegness beach of Lincolnshire Poacher after she had arrived on station, 31 July 1990. (Jeff Morris)

Rev Stephen Holmes of Skegness Parish
Church, the Rev Norman Walker and the
Rev Father Joseph Finneran. The lifeboat
was christened by Mrs Van Geest with a
bottle of champagne smashed over her
bows, after which she was launched with
several guests aboard, and put through her
paces for a short demonstration to those
both ashore and afloat.

Before she had been named, *Lincolnshire
Poacher* had completed her first service.
She was launched at 2.15am on 17
August 1990 to search for an RAF

Tornado aircraft missing between Norfolk
and Flamborough Head. The lifeboat
proceeded at full speed to the scene and,
when eleven miles east of Spurn Head,
joined nine other surface craft, including
the Bridlington and Humber lifeboats,
the latter acting as on-scene commander.
Helicopters and a Nimrod aircraft were
also searching. Although some small pieces
of aircraft wreckage were found, there
was no trace of the aircrew, so the three
lifeboats were released from the search,
which continued under the command of

Lincolnshire Poacher is taken across the beach at the end of her naming ceremony to be launched with invited guests on board. (Nicholas Leach)

Lincolnshire Poacher is readied for launching at the end of her naming ceremony on 30 September 1990. (Nicholas Leach)

the warship *Dumbarton Castle*. *Lincolnshire Poacher* returned to Skegness at 1.50pm having been at sea in near gale force seven winds for more than eleven hours. This first service launch proved a good test for the new boat, as she covered 105 miles and went thirty-five miles from station in moderately rough seas.

The first life-saving service by *Lincolnshire Poacher* took place on 4 November 1990 after a local man was overcome by exhaustion while trying to surf off the central beach. The lifeboat launched at 10.18am and was soon alongside the surfer. He was found to be so weak that, had it not been for a very fast response by the crew on the foredeck, he would have slid off his board and

drowned. However, the crew pulled him, semi-conscious, on board and, in the warmth of the wheelhouse, he was treated for hypothermia. It was low water so, as soon as the boat had beached, the stretcher was transferred to the Talus MB-H tractor in the surf and taken up the beach to the waiting ambulance. The lifeboat had been at sea for only fourteen minutes but the surfboarder, who recovered in hospital, survived thanks to the quick response and teamwork of all the emergency services.

Both lifeboats were involved in a full-scale search on 1 September 1991 after the power boat *Team Traction* was reported overdue from a water ski championship race between Hunstanton and Skegness. During the race visibility was reduced by bad weather and, with conditions made worse by a choppy sea and a north-easterly force four wind, many of the competitors failed to complete the race. By 4pm, *Team Traction*, with three persons on board, was still missing, so the ILB launched to search from Chapel St Leonards to Gibraltar Point and *Lincolnshire Poacher* put out to cover east of Skegness to the central part of the Wash. The Hunstanton lifeboat and an RAF Wessex helicopter, together with Coastguard Auxiliary search teams, were also involved. With nothing found by dusk, the search area was expanded and a Sea King helicopter was tasked. At 8.11pm, the helicopter spotted a red flare to the north-east of Chapel and found the craft. *Lincolnshire Poacher* arrived a few minutes later, took on board a woman and her daughter, and guided the powerboat

Lincolnshire Poacher launching and at sea following her naming ceremony on 30 September 1990. (Nicholas Leach)

The new lifeboat house built in 1990 for the 12m Mersey class lifeboat, pictured on the day it was officially opened. (Nicholas Leach)

Stones laid into the outside walls of the new lifeboat house, commemorating the lifeboat appeal and the construction of the new boathouse. (Nicholas Leach)

THIS STONE WAS LAID BY
COUN. K. J. HOLLAND,
B.E.M.
TOWN MAYOR
AND
FORMER COXSWAIN
JANUARY 1990

THIS STONE WAS LAID BY
J. L. ROUGHTON, ESQ.
C.B.E., D.L., J.P.,
CHAIRMAN OF THE
LINCOLNSHIRE LIFEBOAT
APPEAL FUND
JANUARY 1990

Michael Vernon officially opens the new boathouse during the naming ceremony, 30 September 1990.

back to Hunstanton. The casualty had no compass, chart or radio and, on being asked how he navigated, stated that he followed the other boats.

On 9 June 1992 *Lincolnshire Poacher* was launched to assist the disabled sailing yacht *Chi-Chi* in thick fog east of Skegness. Once at sea, the lifeboat's radar failed so finding the casualty proved more difficult and its position had to be worked out manually. At 12.57pm, more than two hours after launching, the estimated position was reached, the lifeboat having been navigated blind with basic chartwork, and no buoys or navigational marks visible. A bearing was taken using the lifeboat's direction-finding equipment, and the casualty was found close by. Assistant Mechanic Graham Phillips was put aboard, and *Chi-Chi* was taken in tow to Wells harbour. By the time Wells bar was reached, the casualty's fuel system had been partially cleared and she was able to continue under her own power. The Wells ILB escorted *Chi-Chi* up the channel to the town quay, while *Lincolnshire Poacher* turned into the fog for home.

During summer 1992 the ILB launched fourteen times to inflatables blowing out to sea with a near tragedy on 1 August after a young girl was blown seawards on an airbed in force five winds off Ingoldmells. The ILB was quickly launched soon followed by *Lincolnshire Poacher* when

reports indicated that the airbed had
overturned and a swimmer, who had
attempted a rescue, had been lost from
sight. A helicopter from RAF Coltishall
was also tasked and found the child in
the water twenty-five minutes after the
airbed had flipped over. The child was
flown direct to Grimsby hospital and the
lifeboats returned to station.

A worse incident happened on 17
August when the ILB was launched to
check an inflatable blowing out to sea
off Chapel St Leonards. The inflatable
was found to be empty but one of its
occupants, a seventeen-year-old boy, had
swum ashore and another was missing.
Lincolnshire Poacher launched immediately
and an RAF helicopter was scrambled
to join the search between Chapel Point
and Sutton. Mablethorpe ILB was also
involved but, after six hours, the search
was called off with the person still missing.

The last launch of 1992, on 27
December, thoroughly tested both the
power and manoeuvrability of the lifeboat.
Lincolnshire Poacher was launched into
heavy surf in an easterly force five wind to
the fishing vessel *Wash Princess*, of King's
Lynn, aground near Mablethorpe, sixteen
miles north of Skegness, with the Humber

Lincolnshire Poacher is hauled back onto her carriage following the naming ceremony launch, and she is then brought back to the boathouse. (Nicholas Leach)

lifeboat unable to get close enough in the shallow water and heavy surf as her propellers were not protected.

The Skegness boat arrived on scene and manoeuvred into the shallow water inside the surf-line stern first, with her head to sea, and a heavy tow rope was passed to the trawler. The lifeboat cleared the surf before attempting to tow the vessel, which had gone aground at high water with her gear still over the side. The trawler was gradually worked free by the lifeboat, and then pulled through the surf into deeper water. *Wash Princess* was able to proceed under her own power, albeit at slow speed with her gear still over the side, to Grimsby escorted by the Humber lifeboat.

The following year, 1993, was the busiest year for the Skegness lifeboat since the war with the all-weather lifeboat launching twenty times on service. The first service was on 5 January 1993 to the Norwegian coaster *Leopold* which had gone aground on the Long Sand in rough seas and a force seven wind. *Lincolnshire Poacher* launched at 4.08am and soon found the casualty by radar after a rough passage. Although seas were breaking around the ship, she was not in danger when she settled with the falling tide so

the lifeboat stood by until *Leopold* reported that she had taken the ground without damage, and then returned to station. The lifeboat launched again at 12.30pm to assist in floating the coaster off. At high tide, a heavy tow rope was passed to the ship, and the lifeboat helped to pull her into deep water. The undamaged *Leopold* then continued her passage.

The ILB was involved in a very testing service on 25 March 1993. The 23ft fishing boat *Kingfisher* was capsized close inshore at the north end of Skegness after attempting to pass a tow line to the tug *Brenda*. A large breaking wave caught the boat and capsized it, throwing the two crew into the sea. The skipper of the tug raised the alarm and the ILB launched at

Boat's officers in the late 1990s, left to right, were Second Coxswain John Irving, Coxswain Paul Martin and Deputy Second Coxswain Ray Chapman. (By courtesy of Skegness RNLI)

Lincolnshire Poacher heads out through the surf off the beach after launching.

4.40pm. As nobody could be seen either in the heavy surf or on the beach, the ILB immediately requested the support of *Lincolnshire Poacher*. Searching in heavy surf, the ILB was at its operational limits with both boat and crew taking a severe punishment. A Sea King helicopter from RAF Leconfield joined the search, with the two lifeboats working close inshore.

The upturned hull of *Kingfisher* had been washed ashore with no sign of the crew. Another fishing boat joined the search, which continued in the dark until being called off at 8.55pm. The ILB was at sea throughout, except during a crew change, and one of the crew, Mick Abbott, suffered injuries and needed hospital treatment. Sadly, the two fishermen did not survive and their bodies washed up on the beach a few days later. Following this service, a letter of commendation from the RNLI's Chief of Operations was sent to the station thanking the crews of both boats for their efforts, and especially the ILB crew and helmsman John Irving.

On 26 July 1993, the relief lifeboat *Marine Engineer* arrived on station and *Lincolnshire Poacher* went for refit at Crown Fletcher's yard at Oulton Broad, Lowestoft. The relief boat completed four effective services during almost three months at Skegness, the longest of which was the last, on 4 September, when she launched just before 7.30pm to search for an inflatable tender which, with one man on board, had been swept past the anchored 36ft motor yacht *Umphasi* by a strong flood tide. The lifeboat found the yacht dragging its anchor, with another person on board, south of Gibraltar Point, but as it was in no immediate danger started searching for the tender.

As darkness fell, an RAF Sea King helicopter with night vision equipment was scrambled, together with Hunstanton lifeboat, and Wells lifeboat also launched to cover the entrance to the Wash. At one point, the Skegness lifeboat had to leave the search to help *Umphasi*, which was in danger of going ashore. The lifeboat took off the boat's remaining occupant and left the yacht as the search continued throughout the night, but without result. Had the occupant been wearing a lifejacket with reflectors and carrying flares or a torch, he would have

been found earlier than at dawn, when he scrambled ashore near Skegness, exhausted and with blistered hands from rowing. On her way back to the station, *Marine Engineer* towed *Umphasi* clear of the surf, after which two lifeboat crew took her up Wainfleet Haven, escorted by the lifeboat.

On 17 October 1993, *Lincolnshire Poacher* returned to station and *Marine Engineer* was taken to Denton Shiprepairers at Otterham Quay for her own survey before her next relief duty at Dungeness. During 1994 *Lincolnshire Poacher* launched on a number of occasions to help fishing vessels. On 1 June she went to the cockle boat *Girl Mandy* which had capsized in shallow water on the Friskney Flats. Although one man was trapped in the wheelhouse for a while, both crew escaped unhurt, and the boat was saved by the lifeboat's pump which was used to empty the vessel. The pump was used again on 16 November after the Boston fishing boat *Hopeful* began taking in water in Boston Deeps. The lifeboat launched at 12.46pm and found the casualty eight miles off Skegness. The pump was put on board and cleared the water, which was entering through a damaged sea-cock.

On 3 June 1994 a new inshore lifeboat, D-460, was placed on station at Skegness. This boat had been funded by the Leicester Branch of the RNLI. The naming ceremony took place on 30 October and, because of the rain and strong winds, was held inside the boathouse. Derrick C. Young, Chairman of the Leicester Branch, formally handed the boat over to the RNLI and into the care of Commandant Vonla McBride CB BA, Vice-President of the committee of management, who passed her into the care of the Skegness station. Honorary Secretary Joel Grunnill received her on behalf of the station, and the new boat was christened *Leicester Fox* by Mrs Chris Young. After the ceremony the new ILB

Lifeboat crew with Lincolnshire Poacher, from left to right: Rod Bee, Trevor Holland, Gavin Abbott, Ian Johnson, Ray McDermott, Paul Martin, Bob Limb, Mick Clark, Mick Abbott, John Irving, Richard Watson, Brian Porter, Ray Chapman, Brian Wright and Paul Maltby. (By courtesy of Skegness RNLI)

The naming ceremony of the D class inflatable D-460 Leicester Fox inside the lifeboat house on 30 October 1994. (By courtesy of Skegness RNLI)

Assistant tractor driver Rodney Bee, who started in April 1990 and finished in August 2001, with head tractor driver Trevor Holland (on right) in front of the Talus MB-H tractor T117 outside the lifeboat house. (By courtesy of Skegness RNLI)

was launched for a short demonstration of her capabilities.

On 20 December 1994 *Lincolnshire Poacher* went to the Grimsby fishing vessel *Clavis*, which had put out a Mayday after fire broke out on board forcing her two crew took to take to the life-raft. The lifeboat launched at 9.20pm and arrived on scene to find the motor vessel *Serinites* alongside the life-raft with *Clavis* blazing fiercely nearby. The fishing boat's crew were later transferred to Grimsby by

an RAF helicopter as the lifeboat crew, having recovered the life-raft, attempted to put out the fire while awaiting the arrival of the salvage tug *Anglian Duke*. The tug arrived at 2.30am on 21 December and the lifeboat returned to Skegness while *Clavis*, still burning from the fuel oil in the engine room, sank shortly afterwards.

On 15 January 1995 *Lincolnshire Poacher* was launched for what proved to be an unusual service. She put out at 4.50pm after an airship, the 45m twin-engined

The remains of the airship Virgin Star on the beach at Skegness. The 132ft craft was towed fifteen miles before being dragged onto the beach. About twenty lifeboat crew were involved in the operation, after which the remains of the airship were salvaged by Virgin's ground crew. The two crew members on the left are Ray Chapman and John Irving. (By courtesy of Skegness RNLI)

craft named *Virgin Star*, got into difficulty. The airship, which was on a pleasure flight, experienced steering problems over Bedford and was blown by the south-westerly wind to the Wash where the pilot, Captain David Holliholmes, was able to put the airship's gondola down on the bombing range at Holbeach so that most of the people could get off. But the wind then blew the airship out to sea until the pilot managed to ditch the gondola and airship in the Gat Channel area, about sixteen miles from Skegness.

The lifeboat arrived on scene as an RAF helicopter was directing the Sutton Bridge pilot boat onto the half-submerged gondola to take off the pilot. Rather than leave the airship, Coxswain Paul Martin decided to attempt to tow it downwind back to Skegness. This proved to be a very difficult task requiring constant adjustments to the towing bridles to hold a course across the wind and tide and avoid the sandbanks, with the gondola sometimes submerged and sometimes airborne. The arduous tow continued for several hours with the airship settling further in the water. When the tide turned, progress was impossible, so the airship was left on the beach.

On 11 July 1995 *Lincolnshire Poacher* and her crew were involved in a very fine service after the fishing boat *Boy Darren*, of Grimsby, got into serious difficulties in heavy surf close to the sea wall. The lifeboat launched at 4.48am and took just eight minutes to reach the casualty, being told on the way that *Boy Darren* was within minutes of being smashed up. The lifeboat arrived to find the casualty with heavy surf breaking over her, and waves pushing her up the concrete sea wall. One crew man had scrambled ashore, but the

Lincolnshire Poacher on service to the fishing boat Boy Darren on 11 July 1995. (By courtesy of Skegness RNLI)

Pictured from the Humber lifeboat, Lincolnshire Poacher on service to the yacht Breock on 24 July 1996, fifteen miles east-north-east of Skegness. The casualty, with three people on board, was towed to the Humber. (By courtesy of Skegness RNLI)

Lincolnshire Poacher arriving at Lowestoft on passage to Lymington for refit at West Custom Marine, 16 November 1998. (Gary Markham)

Lincolnshire Poacher leaving West Custom Marine at Lymington, 19 March 1999, following her refit. She was taken to Haven Boatyard for trials. (Peter Edey)

Lincolnshire Poacher at Lymington on 19 March 1999 for trials after refit at West Custom Marine. She had her livery slightly altered to conform to the RNLI's new standards, with a yellow and red strip along the hull, and the operational number displayed on the bow rather than the wheelhouse. (Peter Edey)

Five Skegness Coxswains, pictured at the North Shore Hotel, Christmas 2000. The are, left to right, Ken Holland, Joel Grunnill, Ron Chapman, Paul Martin and John Irving. (By courtesy of Ben Hardaker)

other two were still on board the partially swamped boat. Heaving lines and tow ropes with bridles were rigged and the lifeboat was taken stern first into the surf-line, head to sea. At the first attempt the tow was attached, and the lifeboat cleared the surf before the tow was tightened.

The casualty was dragged off, into deeper water, but as she was being towed clear her crew radioed that she was taking on water so the lifeboat went alongside to transfer a portable pump. The tow was resumed while the water was pumped out and the leak was found and stopped. The fishing boat was towed as far as Saltfleet, where she was handed over to the Humber lifeboat to take to Grimsby. The return

of service report stated 'the crew worked very well in a tight and difficult situation where getting it right first time with the ropework was essential'. In recognition of their efforts, a letter of commendation was received from the RNLI's Chief of Operations congratulating the Coxswain for a fine display of seamanship and the crew for their support and teamwork.

Three months after a service on 6 January 1996 to stand by and escort the barge *Gray Mammoth*, which had one of its two propellers fouled by a rope, *Lincolnshire Poacher* was taken to Leggett's boatyard at Grimsby for a routine survey. In her place, on 2 April 1996, came the relief Mersey lifeboat *Her Majesty*

D-460 Leicester Fox returns from exercise, watched by holiday-makers. On board are, left to right, Simon Tasker, Andy Parker, Stephen Johnson, Richard Watson and Kevin Smith. (By courtesy of Skegness RNLI)

The Queen, which stayed until 16 May, performing one service during her short stint at the station. After she returned to station, the first service by *Lincolnshire Poacher* took place on 29 June 1996 when she went to the 32ft motor cruiser *Royal Capers*, with a crew of three, which had lost its steering and was drifting towards Hunstanton. The lifeboat launched at 11am and towed the vessel to King's Lynn.

Between 3 and 10 August 1996, the relief Mersey lifeboat *Peggy and Alex Caird*, the first Mersey class lifeboat to be built and originally stationed at Bridlington, was on station while *Lincolnshire Poacher* went to Leggett's at Grimsby for some minor engine repairs. The relief lifeboat did not perform any services during her week at Skegness, and, on returning, the station lifeboat had a quiet time for the remainder of the year, until called upon on 19 December to perform what proved to be a long service.

She launched at 3.25am to the 55ft motor cruiser *Golden Tarka*, which had got into difficulties about twenty-five miles north-east of Skegness whilst en route from Great Yarmouth to Amble in Northumberland. The cruiser's steering had broken in gale force eight winds,

Lincolnshire Poacher launching on exercise through moderate surf on 19 December 1999 to meet up with Hunstanton lifeboat for the annual Christmas get-together. This was also Paul Martin's last launch as Coxswain. (By courtesy of Skegness RNLI)

and as the lifeboat arrived on scene the weather worsened. Two crew members, Deputy Coxswain John Irving and Assistant Mechanic Ian Johnson, were transferred to the cruiser, despite the difficult conditions, and relieved the casualty's two tired crew. The lifeboat then towed the vessel more than twelve miles, before handing it over to the Humber lifeboat, and returned to station to be recovered.

Lincolnshire Poacher completed a series of routine services during 1997, helping the motor boat *Snoopy* in January, the 30ft motor cruiser *Frances G* in June, which was aground on the Inner Knock, and the yacht *Amigo* in August. On 10 September she towed the Skegness Diving Club's rigid-inflatable boat *Skegness Diver*, and its crew of five, to Jackson's Corner for repairs after the boat's engines had failed. On 7 October, she was called out after the dredger *Ham 312* sucked up an unexploded Second World War bomb while working on a beach replenishment programme off Mablethorpe. The lifeboat stood by to evacuate the dredger's crew, but was not needed as the bomb was put back in the water to be handled by a Royal Navy bomb disposal team.

The dangers of inflatables on the beach were well demonstrated during the year,

with the ILB performing many services to rubber dinghies and airbeds throughout the summer. During the last few days of July 1997, *Leicester Fox* was often out helping rubber dinghies, saving two dinghies and their two occupants on 25 July, and bringing another to safety two days later. On 30 July, the ILB saved four rubber dinghies and an airbed, rescuing no fewer than eight persons during a very busy day.

In mid-August 1997 the ILB assisted more rubber dinghies, and on 21 August brought in three dinghies while saving

The lifeboat house of 1990 with the observation tower, which was added in 1998 on the east side and provided a viewing platform over the beach as well as better ILB crew changing facilities and an additional office. (Nicholas Leach)

Coswain John Irving (on left) and Second Coxswain Ray Chapman. Both were appointed to their respective positions in December 1999 having served on the crew for many years. John joined the crew in February 1985 and served as beach helper, ILB helm and Second Coxswain before becoming full-time Coxswain. (By courtesy of Skegness RNLI)

Skegness lifeboat, relief 12m Mersey Lifetime Care, meeting up to exchange Christmas gifts with Hunstanton lifeboat, Atlantic 75 B-749 DJS, Haverhill, December 1998. (Nicholas Leach)

The crew who took part in the Sea Fever service, April 1998, left to right, were Andrew Epton, David Sellers, Ray McDermott, Nick Abbott and Brian Porter; seated are Richard Watson and Coxswain Paul Martin. (By courtesy of Skegness RNLI)

five persons. However, on 29 August, the ILB, as well as *Lincolnshire Poacher*, was involved in a tragic incident after a twenty-five-year-old man was swept out to sea in his dinghy by the tide and offshore breeze. He was at sea in the blow-up boat off the caravan site at Chapel St Leonards, but was caught out by the conditions. The ILB launched after an alarm call from a member of the public, and *Lincolnshire Poacher* put to sea at 11.12am to assist. The dinghy was eventually recovered ten miles from the beach, but the man was never found. This tragedy demonstrated just how dangerous small inflatables and airbeds can be, if those using them are not aware of the tide and wind.

Lincolnshire Poacher was busier than ever during 1998, performing more than twenty service launches and completing a number of effective services. The most

outstanding and difficult rescue of the year took place on 11 April when she was launched at 7.22pm to go to the yacht *Sea Fever*, which had lost steering twelve miles east of Skegness. The 44ft yacht was in contact with the dredger *Sand Wader*, which was anchored near Scott Patch and was preparing to get underway to render assistance. Only one person was on the yacht, and it had no steering. The lifeboat reached the yacht soon after 8pm and found it yawing violently, with the engine and the jammed steering causing it to sheer to windward in the troughs. The wind was force seven to eight and the steep seas were at times 15ft high.

In the heavy seas, the lifeboat had to make five approaches before a crew member could get across to the yacht, and a further two before a second crew member was aboard. The yacht's skipper was suffering from exhaustion and seasickness, so the lifeboatmen prepared the yacht for towing, stopping the yacht's engine and reducing the casualty's violent motion. The yacht was then taken to Grimsby, the only available harbour at that state of tide, in force six northerly winds at a speed of just over six knots. After five and a half hours of arduous towing, the lifeboat and yacht reached Grimsby Fish Dock where the casualty was moored alongside. The lifeboat then began the long journey home, returning to station in the early hours of the following day, more than nine hours after launching. In recognition of his efforts, and those

Exercise launch of 12m Mersey Lincolnshire Poacher and D class inflatable D-460 Leicester Fox in March 2000. (Nicholas Leach)

Recovery of 12m
Mersey Lincolnshire
Poacher after exercise
in March 2000 using
Talus MB-H tractor T117.
(Nicholas Leach)

The rescue of five fishermen from the fishing vessel Zuiderzee, which had its propellers fouled by its nets on 10 June 2001. (By courtesy of RNLI Skegness)

of the crew, during this difficult service, Coxswain Martin was accorded the RNLI's Thanks Inscribed on Vellum. Crew members Richard Watson, David Sellers, Raymond McDermott, Andrew Epton, Brian Porter and Michael Abbot received Vellum Service Certificates.

Both lifeboats were launched on 8 June 1998 to answer separate calls for help. The ILB searched for a swimmer reported to be in difficulty, and was then diverted to help *Lincolnshire Poacher*, which had gone to the fishing vessel *Hannah Charlotte*, with a crew of two, which was in difficulty three miles north of Chapel St Leonards, in winds rising to force six. Although operating at the limit of her capabilities, the ILB succeeded in getting a tow line to

the casualty, which the all-weather lifeboat then pulled to safety.

The last two services of the year also tested the lifeboat's crew to the limit, and were undertaken in difficult conditions. On 4 October, the lifeboat launched at 4.30pm to the yacht *Puffin*, which was in difficulty nine miles south of Skegness, near Long Sand. The lifeboat reached the casualty, and took it in tow to Gibraltar Point, in choppy seas and a head wind gusting to force seven. The last service of the year was to the 40ft fishing vessel *Wash Princess* on 27 October which was in difficulty in force eight winds and very rough seas. The vessel's wheelhouse windows had been smashed by heavy seas, covering the skipper in broken glass.

Recovery after exercise
of Lincolnshire Poacher
using the Talus MB-H
tractor, with the tractor
used to launch the
ILB and tow the skid
trailer. (By courtesy of
Skegness RNLI)

A helicopter and the Hunstanton lifeboat were standing by when *Lincolnshire Poacher* reached the scene. She escorted the vessel to King's Lynn harbour.

The following month, on 16 November 1998, the relief Mersey lifeboat *Lifetime Care* took up duty while *Lincolnshire Poacher* went for refit, and the relief boat performed three services while at Skegness. The first, on 24 January 1999, was to a crewman who had severely damaged his hand on board the fishing vessel *Portunus*, three and a half miles from Skegness. The lifeboat launched at 9.19pm into heavy seas, with force seven winds and a three metre swell. Three attempts had to be made by the lifeboat to get alongside the fishing vessel so that the injured crewman could get across to the lifeboat. Some deck fixtures and rails were torn from the lifeboat during the transfer, but the injured crewman was got aboard safely for a brief, but rough, trip back to Skegness where an ambulance took him to Boston and then to Derby hospital. The Honorary Secretary's report concluded: 'this service was extremely well carried out by Coxswain Martin and the crew in extreme, violently rough conditions'.

On 6 April 1999, *Lifetime Care* was

Lincolnshire Poacher
launching for lifeboat
day 2003. (Ben
Hardaker, courtesy
of Skegness RNLI)

Watched by a crowd of holiday-makers, Lincolnshire Poacher is launched for lifeboat day 2003. (Ben Hardaker, courtesy of Skegness RNLI)

Lincolnshire Poacher at sea for lifeboat day 2003. (Ben Hardaker, courtesy of Skegness RNLI)

involved in a major operation, along with the inshore lifeboat *Leicester Fox*, Mablethorpe ILB, the police, Coastguards and Rescue helicopter 128, after an inflatable dinghy was blown out to sea off Huttoft, nine miles north of Skegness. One of the two girls in the dinghy managed to make it ashore, but, despite the massive search, with Skegness' two lifeboats searching for almost five hours, the other girl was not found in time. A few days after this tragedy, on 11 April 1999,

Lincolnshire Poacher returned to station. She had undergone an extensive overhaul at West Custom Marine, Lymington, with new laser plotter navigational equipment fitted at a cost of £11,000.

Lincolnshire Poacher performed several services during 1999 following her return from overhaul. On 22 August, she launched at 10.31am to investigate reports that smoke had been seen coming from the fishing vessel *Lady Joan* off Chapel St Leonards. Although the smoke was

On board Lincolnshire Poacher during lifeboat day 2003. Standing, left to right, John Irving, Rev Ian Banks and Graham Phillips; Ron Chapman in middle; and seated are Joel Grunnill and Ken Holland. (Ben Hardaker, by courtesy of Skegness RNLI)

Two photos of the Massey Ferguson agricultural tractor TA40 which has been on station since 1999. It is used to launch the ILB (below, in 2000) and tow the skid trailer (right, in 2008) during the recovery procedure. In 2006 the vehicle was overhauled and repainted in dark blue. (Nicholas Leach)

coming from the vessel's shrimp boiler, the crew was having difficulty with the vessel's engines so the craft was towed to King's Lynn. *Lincolnshire Poacher* towed another vessel, the 25ft yacht *Alican*, on 23 September 1999, launching at 4.17am to help the craft which was in difficulty off Gibraltar Point with three people on

board. The lifeboat located the yacht, which was from Scarborough, and two crew went aboard to assist with a tow towards Boston.

During 2000, a number of routine towing services were completed by *Lincolnshire Poacher*. The first was on 26 March after the fishing vessel *La Belle Ilenne* suffered engine failure about seventeen miles north-east of Skegness, and so was towed to Grimsby. On 28 August the lifeboat went to the powerboat *Snodgrass*, aground on the Seal Sand eighteen miles south-east of Skegness, and towed it off at high tide. On 24 September both lifeboat and ILB went to the disabled yacht *Carpadium* and towed it to Wainfleet Haven, where it was anchored, and its two crew were brought back to Skegness.

Three days later, *Lincolnshire Poacher* went to the 36ft motor vessel *Wild Rover*, which had run aground near the Woolpack Buoy, nine miles from Skegness, in force eight winds. The lifeboat was taken alongside the casualty to transfer a crew man, who connected and manned the tow line during a slow and difficult passage to King's Lynn in heavy weather. The final service of the year took place on 7 October when the lifeboat launched at 9.46pm to the 52ft fishing vessel *Buzzard*, a beam trawler, which had broken down nine miles south-east of Skegness. The vessel was towed to King's Lynn.

The all-weather lifeboat's first service in 2001 was on 10 June when she went to the seventy-six-ton fishing vessel *Zuiderzee*, which, in force eight winds and deteriorating conditions, was disabled with gear around her propellers. The vessel's crew of four dropped anchor to prevent the craft from drifting onto sandbanks, and then radioed for help. The lifeboat launched just after 2pm and reached the scene to find the beam trawler without power, Rescue helicopter 128 and Hunstanton lifeboat standing by, and the coaster *Gerhein G* also on scene. The lifeboat went alongside the casualty to pass across a tow rope, took the vessel in tow and headed for the river Nene. Here, the tug *Fenlander* took over the tow and *Lincolnshire Poacher* returned to station, arriving on the beach after 10pm having been at sea for eight hours. Later in the year, on 16 October, the lifeboat again

Launch of Lincolnshire Poacher with Talus MB-H tractor T117 on a medical exercise in 2004. (Ben Hardaker, courtesy of Skegness RNLI)

went to the aid of *Zuiderzee*, which was in difficulty this time with engine trouble off Mablethorpe. The lifeboat, already on exercise, stood by while the Humber lifeboat took the fishing vessel in tow.

During the afternoon of 29 July 2001, both Skegness lifeboats were involved in numerous incidents after a strong offshore wind caught out holiday-makers using inflatables on the beach. The hot sun brought out thousands of people, and when the wind picked up many in the water were blown out to sea. The lifeboats were called out for what proved to be the busiest afternoon in the station's history. The inshore lifeboat *Leicester Fox* was launched at 1.23pm and began getting the inflatables to safety, with the all-weather lifeboat getting afloat at 1.53pm. Jet skis and a broken-down speedboat were also brought to safety, with the lifeboat returning to station at 5.20pm and the ILB not getting back until almost 7pm having saved or assisted at least forty people.

Two days later, one of the lifeboat crew, Andrew Parker, aged eighteen, was involved in a single-handed rescue for which he received considerable praise. At around 8pm two boys, aged ten and thirteen, were playing at Ingoldmells when they fell into the sea. A man, Mark Walsh, and his family were passing the scene and Walsh had no hesitation in going into the sea to rescue the boys, but he in turn got into difficulties. Off-duty lifeboatman

Parker was passing with his father and went into the sea after the three people. First he reached the thirteen-year-old and pulled him to shore before going back for the other two. As Parker went back for the ten-year-old boy, he saw that Walsh was under water, so grabbed both him and the boy to bring them out of the sea at the same time.

Although none of the crowd of onlookers went to help Andrew, he continued his efforts to save Walsh by giving mouth-to-mouth resuscitation. An ambulance arrived, and coastguards helped with resuscitation but Walsh was pronounced dead at Skegness Hospital. The rescue was later hailed as a 'superhuman effort' by Honorary

On his retirement as Honorary Secretary in 2005, Peter Newsome (centre right) is presented with a certificate of service by Divisional Inspector Andrew Ashton. Also at the ceremony were Joel Grunnill (on left), and Alan Fisher, the current Lifeboat Operations Manager. (Ben Hardaker, courtesy of Skegness RNLI)

Relief 12m Mersey lifeboat Fishermen's Friend launching on exercise through moderate surf in February 2004. (By courtesy of Ben Hardaker)

Lincolnshire Poacher returns from refit at Lymington, May 2004, with the relief lifeboat Fishermen's Friend being prepared for launching. Lincolnshire Poacher was brought back to Skegness via the Isle of Wight, an overnight stay at Eastbourne, then across the Channel to Boulogne and back via Ramsgate, Harwich and Lowestoft. She stopped at Wells before the final leg of the journey to Skegness. (By courtesy of Skegness RNLI)

Secretary Peter Newsome, and Parker was awarded a Jolly Fisherman statuette, presented by Skegness Mayor, Councillor Sue Binch. He also received a community award from Skegness Rotary Club, the Scouting Bronze medal for bravery and an award from the Royal Humane Society.

The final service of 2001 took place on 3 November when *Lincolnshire Poacher* was launched just after 9pm to go to the 37ft motor vessel *Star*, which had developed mechanical problems approximately thirteen miles north-east

of Skegness. The vessel's engine was overheating so her skipper called for help. The lifeboat crew reached the vessel within an hour and the lifeboat took her, with her three crew, in tow to Grimsby Fish Docks. Although this was a fairly routine call, the lifeboat crew were at sea for almost eight hours and did not return until 5am the following morning.

On 20 February 2002, a new inshore lifeboat was delivered to the station to replace *Leicester Fox* which had been in service since 1994. The new boat, D-573,

had orange-coloured sponsons unlike her predecessor, which had been mainly grey, and was named *Leicester Fox II*. The new ILB was formally named and dedicated at a ceremony on 7 September. The ceremony was formally opened by Station Chairman Joel Grunnill, and Leicester Branch Chairman Derrick Young handed the boat over to the RNLI and into the care of the station. Leicester Branch souvenir secretary Rosemary Nash-Smith formally christened the new boat, which was then launched for a brief demonstration off the beach.

After a couple of launches that proved to be false alarms, the new ILB was taken

away from station for some minor repairs to be replaced by relief ILB D-425. The new ILB returned to station for the summer and her first effective service took place on 21 July 2002, when she

Rosemary Nash-Smith names the new inshore lifeboat Leicester Fox II on 7 September 2002. (Ben Hardaker, courtesy of Skegness RNLI)

D class inflatable inshore lifeboat Leicester Fox II on exercise, with Matt Jackson at the helm and crew Tony Kelly on the port side (nearest camera) and Gemma Wheelan on the starboard side. (Nicholas Leach)

Skegness lifeboat crew pictured in 2002 outside the lifeboat house. Standing, left to right, are Paul Maltby, Brian Porter, Dave Sellers, Andy Epton, Ian Johnson, Ray Chapman, John Irving, Steve Jackson, Trevor Holland, Mick Clarke, Tim Waite. At the front, left to right, are Ray McDermott, Steve Wymer, Gavin Abbott, Tom McNally, Mick Abbott, Richard Watson, and Mark Holley. (By courtesy of Skegness RNLI)

Skegness inshore lifeboat crew 2002, left to right, Tom McNally, Richard Watson, and Gavin Abbott. (By courtesy of Skegness RNLI)

saved three men in difficulty off North Beach. The men had launched a triple seat jet-ski at Jackson's Corner but were thrown off, and spent two hours in the sea. One of the three had no life-jacket, and by the time the ILB reached them, they were becoming exhausted and suffering hypothermia. One of the lifeboat crew, Simon Tasker, also a council lifeguard on Skegness Central Beach, swam out as the alarm was raised and reached one of the three men. He stayed with the man until the ILB pulled them both from the sea. The ILB crew saved the other two men, who had drifted a quarter of a mile south.

Although suffering from exhaustion, the men were unharmed except for one who had a leg injury.

The most testing service of 2002 took place on 5 May when the Sabre class yacht *Wing* went aground on the northern edge of the Long Sands in force six winds and rough seas. The lifeboat launched just after 9am and soon reached the casualty. After several attempts to get the lifeboat alongside, it was decided to fire a rocket line across to the casualty but the skipper was too exhausted to haul the tow line across, so a final attempt was made to get the lifeboat closer to the yacht. This time,

Lincolnshire Poacher in Lowestoft in May 2004 during her passage to station after refit at Souter Shipyard, Cowes, Isle of Wight. She called in at Southampton, Ramsgate and Lowestoft, before heading to station. On board are, left to right, John Irving, Brian Porter, Peter Newsome (Honorary Secretary), Micky Abbott (seated), Andrew Epton, Ray Chapman (Second Coxswain) and David Sellers (Assistant Mechanic). (By courtesy of Skegness RNLI)

Third Mechanic Dave Sellers leapt across to the casualty with the tow line.

As soon as this was attached, the lifeboat was able to slowly pull the yacht off the sandbank and set course for Boston. The skipper was tired and confused, having not slept for over forty-eight hours. Following this service, Coxswain Irving was sent a letter of commendation from the RNLI Chairman Peter Nicholson, who wrote: 'Your boat handling and seamanship were first class and your prompt reactions to the situation contributed to this successful service'. Dave Sellers received a letter from the RNLI Chief Executive commending his 'selfless action boarding the yacht and assisting the yachtsman'.

On 9 November 2002, the relief Mersey *Peggy and Alex Caird* arrived at the station while *Lincolnshire Poacher* went for refit. The relief boat performed one service during her six-week stay at Skegness, and it proved to be a testing one. In the early hours of 14 November, the fishing vessel *Portunis* ran aground with nets around her propellers and three people on board. At 2.21am, in very rough seas and force seven to eight winds, the lifeboat launched and set course for the casualty.

Once on scene, the lifeboat was able to get close enough to connect a tow at the first attempt and then towed the vessel towards Boston. The lifeboat had to wait at anchor for four hours because of the tide before being able to tow *Portunis* into Boston itself. At Boston the lifeboat was met by the Divisional Inspector Andrew Ashton, as well as the Divisional Engineer Brian Jackson and Divisional Technician Andy Rodgers who inspected the boat and crew on the return passage. The boat was recovered just after 1pm having been out for the best part of twelve hours.

The lifeboat house of 1892-3 remains standing and has been used as a shop called Smuggler's Den. (Nicholas Leach)

Lincolnshire Poacher on service to the yacht Molly Louise on 12 August 2006, working with the Humber lifeboat Pride of the Humber. She launched at 5.35pm to help search for three persons swept overboard from the yacht. The lifeboat crew had to contend with rough seas and force eight to nine winds during a difficult service. The Humber lifeboat took the yacht in tow to Grimsby and the Skegness boat returned to station at 11.20pm. (By courtesy of Skegness RNLI)

Lincolnshire Poacher returned from refit on 18 December 2002 and performed her next service on 20 February 2003, after a call from Yarmouth Coastguard was received stating that an object had been sighted in the sea off Butlins. The lifeboat launched just after 9am and soon established that the object was a 9ft dory, with no sign of any persons in the vicinity. The lifeboat crew brought the boat ashore and recovered the boat, while Coastguards searched the local launch areas for a trailer, but found nothing.

The weekend of 14-15 June 2003 proved to be particularly busy for both Skegness lifeboats. The first call came at 9.42am on 14 June after an airbed was seen drifting off Ingoldmells. *Leicester Fox II* launched to investigate, but the object turned out to be a football. The ILB was called out again at 4.44pm to a jet ski which had broken down off Winthorpe. The ILB towed the craft to Jackson's Corner. The most difficult incident of the weekend took place in the early hours of 15 June after a man in his early thirties was reported in the water off the beach. The ILB crew approached the man, who was behaving aggressively, refusing any assistance and threatening to kill himself and anyone who came near him.

Following attempts by Senior Helmsman Richard Watson to persuade the man to return to shore, it was agreed

12m Mersey Lincolnshire Poacher launching on exercise with crew in position to release the quarter stopper chains as the boat is pushed into the water. (Nicholas Leach)

Skegness lifeboats 2008: 12m Mersey Lincolnshire Poacher and D class inflatable Leicester Fox on exercise. (Nicholas Leach)

12m Mersey Lincolnshire Poacher on exercise near the Lynn Well Windfarm with, left to right, Mark Holley, Ian Johnson, Brian Porter, Richard Watson, Coxswain John Irving at the helm, Ray Chapman, Mike Irving and David Sellers. (Nicholas Leach)

that reinforcements were needed and so *Lincolnshire Poacher* was launched. She stood by for twenty minutes before getting close enough to the man for four crew members, in dry suits, to jump in and overwhelm him. He was then brought aboard the lifeboat and taken ashore to the police. The official press release commented: '. . . the incident shows what crews have to put up with when serving in what is a voluntary service'.

During the first few months of 2004, the relief Mersey lifeboat *Fishermen's Friend* was on station and she performed two services, both to fishing vessels. The first was on 30 March when she launched just after 4.30am to the fishing vessel *Lady Marike*, which had two crew on board and was taking on water and listing heavily ten miles south of Skegness. During passage to the casualty, the lifeboat crew was informed that the vessel had sunk and that the crew had taken to their liferaft. The crew and liferaft were picked up by the fishing vessel *John Willy*, and the lifeboat checked for debris and pollution before returning to Skegness. Her other service took place on 24 April when she towed

12m Mersey Lincolnshire Poacher on exercise. (Nicholas Leach)

Recovery of Lincolnshire Poacher after exercise using Talus MB-H tractor T114, which is the third such tractor to serve the station and arrived in August 2006. (Nicholas Leach)

the fishing vessel *Our Roseanne* towards the Humber and transferred the two crew to the Humber lifeboat. During summer 2004, the relief D class inflatable D-450 *Anthony* was on station, and she undertook a number of launches, all of which were routine in nature.

Most of the services during 2005 involved towing in broken-down vessels. On 28 April *Lincolnshire Poacher* launched at 2.05pm in moderate south-westerly force four winds to the broken-down fishing vessel *Galwad-y-Mor*, twenty-four miles north-east of Skegness. The vessel, with six people on board, was taken in tow

to Grimsby, and the lifeboat returned to Skegness at 11pm. On 12 June she went to the broken-down cabin cruiser *Revels*, in trouble in the Wash south of Wainfleet Haven. Two lifeboat crew were put aboard the vessel to attach a tow, and proceeded towards Boston where the motor cruiser *Daydream* took over the tow. On 22 July *Lincolnshire Poacher* was involved in a long service, launching at 7.45am to the fishing vessel *Seiont A* which had broken down forty miles north-east of Skegness. The casualty was taken towards the Humber, where the Humber lifeboat took the tow.

In the early hours of 4 July 2006, *Lincolnshire Poacher* was launched to assist the motor fishing vessel *Lynn Princess*, which was sinking in the Wash. The lifeboat crew arrived on scene to find the vessel listing to starboard, and Hunstanton Atlantic 75 lifeboat and the fishing vessel *Boy Neil* alongside. A salvage pump, along with two crewmen, was transferred across to pump the water out of the casualty's forward hold, and a tow line was attached.

The vessel was towed onto the Friskeney flats, and with the tide ebbing she settled in shallow water. The tow was disconnected so the lifeboat could get to deeper water, at which point the skipper had the leak under control. Hunstanton

lifeboat took the crewmen off *Lynn Princess*, the pump was left on board, and *Lincolnshire Poacher* returned to station, arriving at 4am. After refuelling, the lifeboat put out again, at 9.30am, and returned to *Wash Princess* to ensure that she refloated, after which the casualty was escorted to King's Lynn, her home port.

Services during 2007 consisted of a variety of casualties, including the usual fishing vessels and yachts getting into difficulty. On 8 May, *Lincolnshire Poacher* was on a routine exercise with

RNLI inspectors on board when she was diverted to a stranded motor cruiser with engine failure. The vessel, *Leo Magill*, was towed to moorings at King's Lynn. During the afternoon and evening of 11 July, *Lincolnshire Poacher* and her crew were called out twice.

The first launch was to the fishing vessel *Sand Kat* which had a faulty radio set that was permanently transmitting on channel 16, thus blocking the emergency channel. The second launch, at 8.15pm, was to a cable-laying rig anchored off Skegness

Skegness lifeboat 12m Mersey Lincolnshire Poacher heads out into the North Sea on exercise. (Nicholas Leach)

on board which one of the workers was injured. The lifeboat took out Dr Sharrock and transferred him to the rig for an initial assessment of the injured man. As he needed further treatment, the casualty was transferred on board *Lincolnshire Poacher* and landed on the beach where an ambulance was waiting.

The first service of 2008 was on 2 February when *Lincolnshire Poacher* launched at 3.43pm after being asked to

help the 9m rigid-inflatable boat *Titan* which had lost steerage and was unable to return to port. The Trinity House vessel *Patricia* provided assistance to *Titan* before the lifeboat arrived. Once the lifeboat was on scene, she took up the tow and headed into the Humber, where it was passed to the Humber lifeboat *Pride of the Humber* shortly after 6pm, and *Lincolnshire Poacher* returned to station to be refuelled and made ready for service.

Appendices

1 • Lifeboats

On station (Launches/ lives saved)	ON	Name Donor	Length Breadth Depth	Type Power Cost	Year (Yard no) Builder	Notes Disposal
1830 – 1864 (50/63)	—	[Not named] RNIPLS Funds and Lincolnshire Coast Shipwreck Association.	24' 8' 3'	Plenty 8 oars £130	1825 William Plenty Newbury	Operated by the Lincolnshire Coast Shipwreck Association Broken up 1864
Oct 1864 – April 1874 (12/34)	—	Herbert Ingram Friends of the late Herbert Ingram, MP for Boston.	30' 7'3" 3'7"	Self-righter 8 oars £219	1864 Forrestt Limehouse	Returned to London 1874
April 1874 – Dec 1888 (23/27)	—	Herbert Ingram Friends of the late Herbert Ingram, MP for Boston.	33' 8' 4'2"	Self-righter 10 oars £295	1866 Forrestt Limehouse	Sold 1888
Dec 1888 – March 1906 (14/13)	203	Ann, John and Mary Legacy of Miss Ann Ball, London.	37' 8' 4'3"	Self-righter 12 oars £594 10s 0d	1888 D. & W. Henderson Partick	Broken up 1906
March 1906 – Dec 1932 (21/21)	554	Samuel Lewis Gift of Mrs Ada Lewis-Hill, 16 Grosvenor Square, London.	35' 10' 4'2"	Liverpool 12 oars £956 1s 9d	1906 (TK 92) Thames Ironworks Blackwall	Sold 1932 and used as pleasure boat at Skegness up to the mid-1960s
Dec 1932 – Dec 1953 (120/43)	760	Anne Allen Legacy of Mrs Anne Allen, Spalding, Lincolnshire.	35'6" 10' 4'6"	Liverpool (M) Single 35hp £3,340 6s 6d	1932 Thornycroft Chiswick	Sold 1953 and converted into fishing boat; subsequently restored at Sutterton
Dec 1953 – April 1964 (48/11)	833	The Cuttle Legacy of Miss F. L. Cuttle, Rotherham, Yorkshire.	35'6" 10'3" 4'6"	Liverpool (M) Single 35hp £4,443 12s 11d	1940 Groves & Guttridge Cowes	At Filey 1940–53 Sold April 1966 for £750 to J. W. Flowers
April 1964 – August 1990 (165/96)	977 (37-10)	Charles Fred Grantham Legacies of Mrs E. W. Montford and Miss E. M. Dearden.	37' 11'6"	Oakley (M) Twin 52hp £33,000	1964 Groves & Guttridge Cowes	Used in Relief Fleet Scrapped at Ridge 20 Aug 1993
7 August 1990 –	1166 (12-008)	Lincolnshire Poacher Van Geest Trust and the Lincolnshire Lifeboat Appeal.	38' 12'6" 6'6"	Mersey (M) Twin 285hp £460,212	1990 Aluminium SB/ Souter, Cowes	

(M) indicates motor lifeboat

2 • Inshore lifeboats

On station (Launches/saved)	ON	Name Donor	Length Breadth	Type Year built	Notes
June – July 1964 (5/3)	D-15	— —	15'3" 6'3"	RFD PB16 1964	
July 1965 – Oct 1972 (61/15)	D-58	— —	15'3" 6'3"	RFD PB16 1965	Transferred to Relief Fleet and Withernsea
March 1973 – Jan 1987 (281/83)	D-212	— Coleshill (Warcs) Carnival Committee.	15'3" 6'3"	RFD PB16 1973	Transferred to Relief Fleet
Jan 1987 – June 1994 (115/38)	D-326	Michel Philippe Wolvers Family of Michel Philippe Wolvers.	16'3" 6'7"	Avon EA16 1987	Transferred to Larne
3 June 1994– Feb 2002	D-460	Leicester Fox Appeal by the Leicester Branch.	16'3" 6'7"	Avon EA16 1994	Transferred to Relief Fleet
20 February 2002–	D-573	Leicester Fox II Appeal by the Leicester Branch.	16'3" 6'7"	Avon EA16 2002	

D-326 Michel Philipe Wolvers. She served from January 1987 for just over seven years. (By courtesy of Ben Hardaker)

D-573 Leicester Fox II. Placed on station in February 2002, she is the second Skegness inshore lifeboat to be funded by the RNLI's Leicester Branch. (Nicholas Leach)

3 • Summary of lifeboat services

First Lifeboat

1833	Aug 31	Brig Hermione, of London, saved 10
1834	Oct	Sloop Resolution, of Wells, saved 3
1838	Jan 24	Sloop Boyne, of Goole, saved 2
1839	Apr 9	Skiff Anna Margueretta, of Hamburg, saved 4
1841	Nov 8	Jane, of Wisbech, saved 3
1844	Feb 27	Steamship City of Carlisle, saved 15
1846	May 3	Speed, of Boston, saved vessel
1848	Oct 13	Galliot Anna Maria, of Bremen, saved vessel
1849	Oct 8	Robert and Mary, saved vessel and 3
1850	Oct 7	Sloop Providence, of Spalding, saved 3
1852	Dec 27	Schooner William, of Lynn, saved 4
1854	Oct 18	Brig Atlanta, of Shields, saved 11

Herbert Ingram Lifeboat

1865	Oct 20	Ketch Grouse, of Wells, services refused
1867	Dec 2	Sloop Ant, of Boston, saved 2
	3	Schooner Elizabeth, of Louth, landed Captain
1869	Jan 17	Ship Stranger, of Boston, services not required, casualty assisted by a steamer
	Oct 19	Brig Unity, of Whitby, could not reach vessel
1871	Sep 30	Brig Regina, of London, saved 7
		Brig Orb, of Whitby, saved 7
		Brig Orb, of Whitby, (second service) saved vessel
		Brig James, of London, services not required
1873	Nov 9	Billiboy schooner Beolitude, of Middlesborough, put off but vessel sank
	10	Barque Françoise Marie, of Caen, and brig Die Schwalbe, of Rostock, assisted to save vessels and 17
1874	Mar 19	Sloop New Eagle, of Grimsby, rendered assistance

Herbert Ingram (second) Lifeboat

1874	Dec 11	Brig Adolphe, of Rochefort, services declined
1875	Apr 9	Dutch galliot schooner Johann. services not required
	Nov 19	Boat of sloop Concord, of Goole, could not find casualty
	Dec 5	Barge Star, of Colchester, saved 3
1876	Apr 14	Ketch Elizabeth, of Goole, saved 2
1877	Jan 30	Sloop Milton Hill, of Lynn, services not required as a passing smack had taken the vessel in tow
1878	Mar 8	Schooner Henry, of Whitby, assisted to save vessel
1879	Jan 19	Sloop Promise, of Boston, assistance not needed
1880	Sep 14	Schooner Luna, of Sunderland, no services rendered, towed to Lynn with the aid of a smack
	Oct 29	A brig and other vessels, no services rendered
1881	Jan 20	Brig Matilda, of Gothenburg, assisted to save vessel
	Oct 23	Barge Lom, of Hudiksval, saved 10
1883	Sep 30	Sloop Good Intent, of King's Lynn, rendered assistance
	Dec 12	Steamship Victoria, of Goole, saved 4
1885	Feb 7	Schooner John Lee, of Blakeney, rendered assistance
1886	Jan 8	Smack Pet, of Grimsby, rendered assistance
1887	Oct 25	Sloop Unity, of Boston, rendered assistance
1888	Jan 28-9	Brig Starbeam, of Boston, saved vessel and 8
	Nov 21	Sloop New Superior, of Boston, rendered assistance

Ann, John and Mary Lifeboat

1890	Apr 8	Sloop Watson, of Goole, saved 4
1892	Nov 2	Fishing dandy, of Grimsby, no service
1893	Nov 19	Fishing smack Frank, of Grimsby, saved 7
	20	Brigantine Vecta, of Harwich, no service
1894	June 17	Three-masted schooner Tataiva, of Riga, no service
1895	Apr 2	Brigantine Camilla, of Laurvig, saved vessel
	Aug 5	Barque Ilma, of Abo, no service
1897	Nov 29	Ketch John Lee, no service
1899	July 29	Smack Daisy, of Wainfleet Haven, landed 1 from the steamship Cam, of Lynn
1905	Jan 6	Small fishing boat, saved 2
1906	Feb 10	Steamship Review, of London, no service

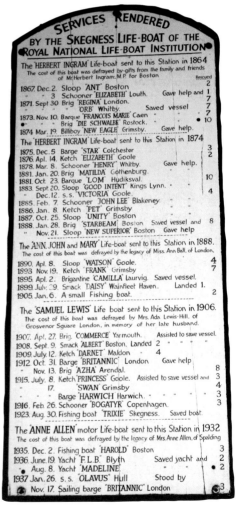

One of the service boards displayed inside the lifeboat house listing the effective rescues carried out by the pulling boats. (Nicholas Leach)

Samuel Lewis Lifeboat

1907	Apr 27-8	Brig Commerce, of Yarmouth, assisted to save vessel and 1
1908	Sep 9	Smack Albert, of Boston, landed 2 and assisted to save vessel in two launches
1909	July 12	Ketch Darnet, of Maldon, landed 4
1912	Oct 31	Barge Britannic, of London, stood by and gave help
	Nov 13	Brig Azha, of Arendal, saved 8
1913	Apr 6	Barque Josua, of Arendal, no service
	June 9	Schooner Paulus, of Panama, no service
1915	July 8-9	Ketch Princess, of Goole, saved 3
	17-8	Ketch Swan, of Grimsby, saved 4
		Barge Harwich, of Harwich, assisted to save vessel and 3
1916	Feb 8-9	Seaplane east of Chapel Point, no service
	Feb 26	Schooner Bogatyr, of Copenhagen, saved 3
1919	Mar 21	Schooner Europa, of Amsterdam, lifeboatmen saved 8 by ropes, lifeboat not launched
1923	Aug 30	Fishing boat Trixie, of Skegness, saved drifting boat
1924	Feb 9	Ketch Aubrey, of Faversham, no service
	Oct 22	Barge Royalty, of Rochester, no service
1927	May 4	RAF aeroplane, no service
1931	Apr 9	Motor boat The Favourite, of Skegness, no service

Anne Allen Lifeboat

1935	Dec 2	Motor fishing boat Harold, of Boston, saved 3
1936	June 19	Yacht F.L.B., of Blyth, saved yacht and 2
	Aug 7	Yacht Madeline, saved yacht and 2
1937	Jan 26	Steamship Olavus, of Hull, stood by
	Nov 17	Barge Britannic, of London, saved 3
1938	Aug 2	Motor fishing boat Blanche, of Cleethorpes, landed 1
	Oct 16	Motor boat Sea Scout, gave help
	Nov 23	Steam drifter Dusty Miller, of Yarmouth, saved 3
1940	Oct 28	British aircraft, picked up a body
1941	Jan 13	Steamship Greyfriar, of Newcastle, gave help
	Feb 15	British aircraft, salved wreckage
	Oct 11	British aircraft, salved a rubber dinghy and saved 5
1942	Jan 9	Steam tug Arcadia, of London, gave help
1943	Jan 21	Two British aircraft, picked up two bodies
	May 21	Netherland Government motor vessel Zuideshaven, landed an injured man
	June 27	British aircraft, salved two dinghies, gear, and saved 2
1944	Jan 16	Landing craft, landed 3
	July 25	Lancaster aircraft, salved gear
	Aug 20	Steamship VIC 72, of Hull, landed 2
	21	Steamship VIC 72, of Hull, escorted
	Sep 2	RAF Launch, stood by
	Oct 18	Aircraft, salved wreckage
1945	May 13	Motor fishing vessels Mary Iversen and Gadanus (Danish), stood by and gave help
1946	Aug 28	Motor cruiser Silver Spray, of Bridlington, saved craft and 2
1947	Jan 5	Fishing smack Virginia, of Boston, assisted to save smack and 3
1948	June 8	Sailing yacht Venture, of Skegness, gave help
	Oct 12	Fishing boat Albert, of Boston, saved boat and 3
1950	June 28	Rubber dinghy, saved dinghy and 6
	29	Sailing boat, escorted
	July 17	Rubber dinghy and tyre, saved 2
	Oct 7	Yacht Catriona, of Littlehampton, gave help
1951	July 10	Rubber dinghy, saved dinghy and 6
1952	Apr 18	Two aircraft, saved 1

The Cuttle Lifeboat

1953	Oct 27	Motor barge Will Everard, of London, stood by
1954	July 18	Converted ship's boat Venture, saved boat and 2
1955	July 27	Motor yacht Petan, of London, gave help
1956	July 29	Yacht Vagabond, of Peterborough, saved yacht and 2
	Aug 29	Bather, landed a body
1957	July 3	Fishing boat Valeria, gave help
		Launch Mirada, gave help
1958	July 12	Sailing dinghy, saved dinghy and 1
	Sep 27	Yacht Olivia, saved yacht and 1
1959	July 29	Motor vessel Rivergate, of Hull, landed 4
	Oct 4	Fishing boat Our Boys, saved boat and 2
1961	June 18	Dinghy Bluebelle, landed 1
1962	Apr 22	Dinghy, stood by
	Aug 14	Motor boat, gave help
1963	Sep 9	Two dinghies, saved dinghies and 3

Charles Fred Grantham Lifeboat

1964	May 3	Catamaran, saved vessel and 2
		Dinghy, saved dinghy and 2
	Nov 2	Persons stranded on Inner Dowsing lightvessel, landed 4
1965	Jan 15	Lynn Well lightvessel, landed a sick man
	Apr 19	Sloop Hal O' The Wind, saved sloop and 3
	June 5	Cabin cruiser Liz, of Peterborough, saved cruiser and 2
	Oct 10	Motor cruiser Golden Spray, saved cruiser and 3
	Dec 28	Oil rig Sea Gem, stood by
1966	Mar 23	Lynn Well lightvessel, landed an injured man and an RAF medical officer
	May 21	Cabin cruiser Higgy, and dinghy, saved two boats and 5
	Aug 14	Speedboat, saved boat and 3
1967	Jan 1	Dinghy, saved dinghy and 2
1968	Feb 22	Cabin cruiser Alula, saved cruiser and 2
	Mar 14	Speedboat Seaspray, saved boat and 2
	30	Dinghy, gave help
	June 25	Fishing boat Seeker, saved boat and 1
	Aug 31	Yacht Olive Marie, gave help
	Sep 22	Converted ship's boat Zulu, gave help
1969	Jan 4	Inner Dowsing lightvessel, landed a sick man
	Apr 16	Catamaran Determination, saved vessel and 4

Amelia Reserve Lifeboat
On station 9 June to 19 July 1969

No services

Charles Fred Grantham Lifeboat

	Aug 29	Dinghy, saved dinghy and 2
	Nov 9	Speedboat, saved boat and 2
1970	July 18	Inner Dowsing lightvessel, landed a sick man
	19	Motor fishing boat Golden Dawn, gave help
	Aug 16	Catamaran Flying Witch, saved vessel and 5
1971	June 12	Inner Dowsing lightvessel, landed an injured man
	Sep 8	Steam tug Northsider, of Newcastle, landed a sick man

	Oct 25	Fishing boat Anita Anna, of Grimsby, gave help
	Nov 2	Sailing dinghy Black Rose, saved 2
1972	Feb 17	Fishing boat Strey Moy, of Grimsby, saved boat and 2
	June 4	Catamaran Flying Witch, saved 4
	Aug 11	Speedboat Malisa, saved boat and 6
	22	Injured man on board motor vessel Adda, of Hamburg, landed an injured man
	24	Motor vessel Adda, of Hamburg, reboarded injured man
	Nov 1	Motor cruiser Boomerang Two, saved cruiser and 6
		Motor cruiser Boomerang Two, gave help
	Dec 2	Fishing vessel Silver Surf, of Boston, saved boat and 2

Calouste Gulbenkian Relief Lifeboat
On station to 3 December 1972 to 5 August 1973

| 1973 | July 9 | Fishing boat Flying Cloud (BH.190), landed a body |

Charles Fred Grantham Lifeboat

1974	Apr 2	Fishing boat Anina (BCK.119), of Buckie, stood by
	Nov 17	Fishing boat, gave help
1975	June 28	Yacht Marza, saved yacht and 1
	July 16	DUKW, saved craft and 16
	27	Yacht, landed 2
	Aug 9	Cabin cruiser Aquarius, gave help
	Sep 6	Fishing boat Jessie (CN.194), gave help
	Nov 24	RAF Phantom jet aircraft, saved 2
1976	Jan 11	Four canoes, saved two canoes
	April 7	Fishing boat Integrity, of King's Lynn, gave help
	June 29	Fishing boat Dolphin, of King's Lynn, saved boat and 2
1977	Jan 13	Fishing boat Thor, saved 2
	May 16	Yacht Davora, saved yacht and 3
	July 9	Yacht Springtime, saved vessel and 2
	Sep 6	Yacht Jasmina, of Hull, saved yacht and 2

Calouste Gulbenkian Relief Lifeboat
On station 29 September 1977 to 16 April 1978

| 1978 | Jan 8 | Motor boat, gave help |
| | 13 | Dinghy, saved dinghy |

Charles Fred Grantham Lifeboat

	July 5	Yacht, gave help
	Oct 4	Fishing vessel Fair Maid, of King's Lynn, saved 1
1979	July 10	Injured man on board cargo vessel Rubin, took out doctor
	Aug 14	Yacht Xanthe, escorted vessel
		Yacht Mavis M, saved 2

J. G. Graves of Sheffield Relief Lifeboat
On station 15 September to 15 October 1979

No services

Charles Fred Grantham Lifeboat

	Dec 13	Aircraft of USAF, recovered wreckage
1980	Aug 3	Motor cruiser Marco, of Jersey, gave help
	12	Yacht Strumpet, of Hull, gave help
	Oct 24	Sailing dinghy, gave help
1981	Feb 19	Cargo vessel Drie Gebroeders, of Panama, escorted

	Mar 14	Cargo vessel Amsel, of Limassol (Cyprus), gave help
	Oct 16	Injured man on board trawler Boy Stevens, took out doctor and landed an injured man
	27	RN vessel, stood by
1982	Feb 25	Speedboat Lightning, gave help
	May 30	Motor cruiser Gramandy, of Poole, gave help
	Sep 5	Yacht Westie, escorted
	Dec 19	Cargo vessel Cedra Sun, of Gibraltar, escorted
1983	Jan 14	Fishing vessel Angelina, of Boston, in tow of cargo vessel Nautic W, escorted vessels
		Fishing vessel Provider, of Boston, escorted boat

Calouste Gulbenkian Relief Lifeboat
On station 25 July 1983 to 22 July 1984

No services

Charles Fred Grantham Lifeboat

1984	July 24	Helicopter, towed ashore and saved helicopter
	Sep 23	Yacht Herself, gave help
	Nov 3	Dinghy, saved dinghy and 1
1985	Feb 7	Cabin cruiser Lindis, gave help
	Sep 26	Fishing vessel Challenge, escorted
1986	Apr 6	Yacht Sterentjie, saved boat and 1

Four of the service boards for the 1960s to 1990s inside the lifeboat house. (Nicholas Leach)

Mary Joicey Relief Lifeboat
On station 6 Oct 1986 to 26 March 1988

1987	Feb 10	Fishing vessel Lady Joan, of King's Lynn, gave help
	June 6	Sea Cadet launch Falcon, gave help
	July 26	Cabin cruiser Laania, saved boat

Charles Fred Grantham Lifeboat

1988	May 18	Fishing boat, gave help
	June 25	Fishing vessel Ben Lora, of North Shields, gave help
	July 3	Yacht Matilda May, gave help
1989	Mar 4	Fishing vessel Jollydee, escorted
	Apr 19	Fishing vessel Maria Carmen, escorted
	May 29	Fishing vessel Barry Williams, gave help
	July 15	Fishing vessel Morning Flight, gave help
1990	Feb 5	USAF Aircraft, recovered wreckage
	Apr 15	Motor cruiser Lady Rysal, gave help

Lincolnshire Poacher Lifeboat
Arrived at station 31 July 1990

	Aug 17	Aircraft, recovered wreckage
	Nov 4	Sailboard, saved 1
1991	Aug 19	Yacht Raetoria, gave help and saved 3
	Sep 1	Motor boat Sar Diver, saved boat and 3
		Power boat Team Traction, gave help
1992	June 9	Yacht Chi-Chi, gave help
	July 5	Trimaran Cufflinks II, gave help
	17	Fishing vessel Slanjie, gave help
	Aug 15	Yacht Silver Tassie, gave help
	21	Cabin cruiser Bulvan Buccaneer, gave help
	Dec 27	Fishing vessel Wash Princess, of King's Lynn, gave help
1993	Jan 5	Cargo vessel Leopold, gave help
	Apr 16	Fishing vessel Jodie Jane, gave help
	May 23	Yacht Misty, gave help
	June 8	Survey ship Deneb, landed an injured man
	July 24	Cabin cruiser Mister Wind, gave help

Marine Engineer Relief Lifeboat
On station 26 July to 17 Oct 1993

	Aug 11	Cabin cruiser Vashtia, gave help
	23	Fishing vessel, saved boat and 3
	25	Yacht Elsker, gave help
	Sep 4	Motor cruiser Umphasi, saved vessel and 1

Lincolnshire Poacher Lifeboat

	Nov 16	Yacht Dignity of Labour, gave help
1994	May 2	Fishing vessel Fastliner, escorted
	June 1	Fishing vessel Girl Mandy, gave help
	15	Fishing vessel Jodie Jane, saved boat and 2
	Aug 24	Yacht Struie, saved boat and 2
	Sep 10	Injured man on board hopper/dredger Sand Heron, took out doctor and landed an injured man
	Nov 16	Fishing vessel Hopeful, saved boat and 3
	Dec 20	Fishing vessel Clavis, gave help
1995	Jan 15	Twin-engined airship Virgin Star, saved airship, towed to Skegness after ditching in Wash
	May 14	Hopper/dredger rock barge MP 1801, gave help

	July 11	Fishing vessel Boy Darren, saved vessel and 2
	Aug 16-18	Yacht Plain Song, gave help
	22	Fishing vessel Girl Mandy, two persons and craft brought in
	31	Fishing vessel Intrepid, towed vessel to Boston Deeps and saved 2
1996	Jan 6	Utility vessel Gray Mammoth, escorted craft

Her Majesty The Queen Relief Lifeboat
On station 2 April to 16 May 1996

	May 4	Yacht Threo, three persons and craft brought in

Lincolnshire Poacher Lifeboat

	June 29	Motor cruiser Royal Capers, saved craft and 3
	July 24	Yacht Breock, saved craft and 3
	31	Catamaran Fingers Crossed, two and craft brought in

Peggy and Alex Caird Relief Lifeboat
On station 3 to 10 August 1996

		No services

Lincolnshire Poacher Lifeboat

	Dec 19	Motor cruiser Golden Tarka, saved craft and 2
1997	Jan 15	Motor boat Snoopy, craft brought in – saved by another lifeboat
	June 10	Motor cruiser Frances G on Wainfleet Sands, gave help
	Aug 4	Yacht Amigo, one person and craft brought in to Boston
	Sep 10	Rubber dinghy Skegness Diver, landed 5 and craft brought in
	Oct 7	Dredger/sand carrier HAM 312 with suspected incendiary bomb aboard, stood by craft
	Nov 23	Survey vessel Fillibuster, four people and craft brought in
1998	Feb 4	Survey boat Andrews One, two people and craft brought in
	Apr 11	Yatch Sea Fever, towed to Grimsby, saved craft and 1
		Jet ski, saved jet ski
	May 26	Yacht Spellsinger, saved craft and 2
	June 8	Fishing vessel Hannah Charlotte, landed 2 and craft saved
	Aug 19	Inflatable dinghies, gave help
	23	Yacht Capi, escorted craft to Boston approaches
	Sep 14	Sailboard disabled, saved board and 1
	Oct 4	Yacht Puffin disabled in Boston Deeps, saved craft and 1
	27	Fishing vessel Wash Princess in difficulties, escorted craft

Lifetime Care Relief Lifeboat
On station 16 Nov 1998 to 11 April 1999

1999	Jan 24	Injured man on board fishing vessel Portunis, landed an injured man
	Apr 4	Speedboat, four persons and craft brought in

Lincolnshire Poacher Lifeboat

	Aug 5	Missing person, gave help
	22	Fishing vessel Lady Joan, three persons and craft brought in
	Sep 19	Trimaran Sis, three persons and craft brought in
	23	Yacht Alikan, three persons and craft brought in
2000	Mar 26	Fishing vessel La Belle Ilenne, three persons and craft brought in
	Aug 28	Powerboat Snodgrass, landed 3 and craft brought in

Sep 24   Yacht Carpadium, landed 2 and craft brought in

27   Motor vessel Wild Rover, saved craft and 2

Oct 7   Fishing vessel Buzzard, landed 2 and craft brought in

Bingo Lifeline Relief Lifeboat
On station 11 to 23 November 2000

No services

Lincolnshire Poacher Lifeboat

2001	June 10	Fishing vessel Zuiderzee, landed 4 and craft brought in
	26	Yacht Wurzeler, stood by
	July 29	Inflatable dinghy, landed 1 and craft brought in
		Inflatable dinghy, landed 2 and craft brought in
		Multiple incidents, gave help
	Oct 16	Fishing vessel Zuiderzee, stood by
	17	Persons cut off by the tide, gave help
	Nov 3	Powerboat MV Star, three persons and craft brought in
2002	Feb 25	Fishing vessel Bussard, gave help
	Apr 2	Powerboat Petana, four persons and craft brought in
	May 5	Yacht Wing, saved craft and 1
	June 9	Yacht Rolling Stone, one person and craft brought in
	July 28	Various, gave help
	Aug 8	Yacht Dragon, four persons and craft brought in – handed to another lifeboat
	11	Motor cruiser Hannah, two persons and craft brought in
	25	Cabin cruiser After the Storm, escorted craft
	Sep 17	Motor cruiser Pelican, gave help

With Coxswain John Irving at the helm, Lincolnshire Poacher brings in the yacht Wing which had gone aground in rough seas and force five winds on 5 May 2002. (By courtesy of Skegness RNLI)

Peggy and Alex Caird Relief Lifeboat
On station 9 November to 18 December 2002

Nov 14   Fishing vessel Portunus, landed 3 and craft brought in

Lincolnshire Poacher Lifeboat

2003	Feb 20	Rowing boat, craft brought in
	June 15	Person in the water, saved 1
	28	Fishing vessel Whitby Crest, two and craft brought in
	July 14	Fishing vessel Sandra James, three and craft brought in
	Nov 21	Yacht Traumerei, two persons and craft brought in

Fishermen's Friend Lifeboat
On station 19 December 2003 until 10 May 2004

2004	Mar 30	Fishing vessel Lady Marike, gave help
	Apr 24	Fishing vessel Our Roseanne, gave help – commenced tow

Lincolnshire Poacher Lifeboat

	May 16	Fishing vessel Black Jack, gave help – commenced tow
		Yacht Will o' the Wisp, gave help – mechanic assisted
	June 4	Sailing dinghy Jansky, gave help
	July 3	Yacht Jestaire, one person and craft brought in
	22	Rig support vessel Sirious B, landed 1
	31	Powered boat Carolina Moon, saved boat and 4
	Aug 19	Person in danger of drowning, gave help
	29	Yacht Isolde, three persons and craft brought in
	Sep 30	Yacht Arawa, two persons and craft brought in
	Nov 26	Catamaran Broad Blue, two persons and craft brought in
2005	Mar 15	Inflatable dinghy, stood by
	Apr 28	Fishing vessel Galwad-y-Mor, six and craft brought in
	June 12	Powered boat Revels, two persons and craft brought in
	July 22	Fishing vessel Seiont A, landed 3 and craft brought in
	Aug 6	Yacht Florence 2, stood by
	Sep 3	Yacht Floozy, two persons and craft brought in
2006	July 4	Fishing vessel Lynn Princess, gave help
		Fishing vessel Lynn Princess, gave help
	Aug 12	Yacht Molly Louise, stood by
	Sep 10	Fishing vessel Quest, four persons and craft brought in
2007	May 8	Powered boat Leo Magill, two persons and craft brought in
	June 1	Fishing vessel Whitby Crest, two and craft brought in
	July 11	Fishing vessel Sand Kat, gave help
		Cable barge, landed 1
	14	Powered boat, craft brought in
	19	Cable barge, landed 1
	Aug 16	Fishing vessel Lady Nicola, 11 persons and craft brought in
	24	Yacht Grandee, three persons and craft brought in
	Oct 22	Yacht Pavana, gave help
	23	Yacht Pavana, one person and craft brought in
	Dec 20	Fishing vessel Sandcat, gave help
2008	Feb 3	Rigid-inflatable Titan, gave help
	May 9	Dinghy, craft brought in

Both lifeboat and inshore lifeboat service lists are correct as of 31 May 2008.

4 • Summary of inshore lifeboat services

D-15 Inshore Lifeboat

1964	July 19	Sailing dinghy, three persons and craft brought in

D-58 Inshore Lifeboat

1965	July 19	Man overboard from small boat, saved boat
1966	May 21	Cabin cruiser Higgy, landed 2
	22	Cabin cruiser Higgy, gave help
	June 4	Fishing boat, gave help
	July 24	Catamaran, gave help
	Aug 13	HMS Pallister, boarded Captain and Chief Engineer
	14	Speedboat, gave help
	24	Bather, gave help
	Sep 6	Speedboat, gave help
1967	Mar 26	Three sailing dinghies, saved 1 dinghy and 3
	Apr 30	Rubber dinghy, escorted
1968	Sep 7	Speedboat Ilya, saved boat and 2
1969	May 26	Sailing dinghy in tow of yacht, gave help
1970	Sep 4	Sailing dinghy, saved dinghy and 3
1971	May 16	Sailing boat, gave help
	Sep 20	Speedboat, saved boat and 3
1972	June 4	Catamaran Flying Witch, gave help
	18	Sailing dinghy, saved dinghy and 2
	Oct 22	Yacht Pas An-Noila, saved yacht and 2

D-212 Inshore Lifeboat

1973	July 2	Rubber dinghy, saved dinghy and 1
	9	Fishing boat Flying Cloud, gave help
	Aug 7	Dinghy, saved dinghy and 2
	30	Speedboat, gave help
	Sep 29	Fishing boat, saved boat and 3
1974	June 2	Speedboat, saved boat and 2
	9	Sailing dinghy, saved dinghy and 2
	19	Speedboat, saved boat, a dog and 1
	July 5	Police Cadet Rescue Boat, gave help
	6	Pleasure boat, saved boat and 5
	29	Airbed, saved 1
		Swimmer, gave help
	Aug 12	Police Rescue Boat, gave help
	13	Bather, saved 1
		Airbeds, saved 2
	24	Speedboat, saved boat and 2
	Sep 22	Sailing dinghy, saved boat and 2
1975	June 13	Sailing dinghy, gave help
	28	Yacht Marza, gave help
	July 5	Person stranded by tide, saved 1
	9	Canoe, saved canoe and 1
	16	Amphibious vehicle, gave help
	20	Speedboat, saved boat and 1
	27	Yacht, gave help
	Sep 6	Fishing boat Jessie, stood by
	Oct 30	Dinghy, escorted
1976	May 16	Speedboat, saved boat and 2
	30	Speedboat, gave help
	June 29	Fishing boat Dolphin, gave help
	Sep 12	Speedboat, saved boat and 2
1977	May 5	Rescued a bullock from the sea
	July 16	Hovercraft, saved craft and 2
	18	Speedboat, saved boat and 3
1978	July 17	Rubber dinghy, gave help
1979	May 25	Canoe, saved canoe
	27	Speedboat, saved boat

	May 29	Rubber dinghy, saved 2
	July 28	Ingoldmells Police Rescue Boat, gave help
	31	Chapel St Leonards Police Cadet rescue boat, gave help
		Ingoldmells Police rescue soat, gave help
	Aug 2	Rubber dinghy, stood by
	21	Rubber dinghies, gave help
	Sep 4	Rubber dinghy, saved dinghy and 1
1980	Aug 17	Man overboard from speedboat, saved boat
	Sep 7	Two rubber dinghies, saved boats
	Oct 24	Sailing dinghy, saved dinghy
1981	July 11	Speedboat, gave help
	20	Two rubber dinghies, saved two boats
	27	Missing child, gave help
	Aug 14	Rubber dinghy, saved 2
	15	Rubber dinghy, saved 2
	23	Canoe, gave help
	Sep 11	Rubber dinghy, saved dinghy
1982	May 28	Sailboard, saved board and 1
	July 10	Rubber dinghy, saved dinghy and 1
	Aug 10	Rubber dinghy, saved dinghy and 2
		Airbeds, saved 2
	11	Rubber dinghy, saved dinghy and 1
	14	Swimmer, gave help
	17	Three rubber dinghies, saved 3 dinghies and 6
		Airbed, saved 1
		Swimmer, landed 1
	29	Catamaran, gave help
1983	June 11	Rubber dinghy, saved dinghy and landed 2
	12	Rubber dinghy, saved dinghy and 1
	27	Fishing boat, gave help
	July 29	Swimmers, gave help
		Rubber dinghies, gave help
		Airbed, escorted airbed
	Aug 1	Rubber dinghy, saved 1
	15	Two rubber dinghies, saved two boats and 3
		Dinghy, saved dinghy
		Airbeds, gave help
		Rubber dinghy, saved dinghy
	16	Rubber dinghy, gave help
	25	Two swimmers, gave help
	Sep 1	Rubber dinghy, saved dinghy
	4	Sailboard, saved board and 1
	17	Speedboat, escorted boat
1984	June 1	Fishing coble Sea Lover, gave help
	3	Speedboat, saved boat
	July 24	Helicopter, saved 3
	27	Rubber dinghy, saved dinghy
	31	Rubber dinghy, saved dinghy and 1
	Aug 13	Swimmer, gave help
	19	Rubber dinghy, gave help
	28	Two rubber dinghies, gave help
		Rubber dinghy, gave help
	29	Rubber dinghy, stood by boat
	31	Rubber dinghy, gave help
	Sep 18	Sailboard, saved board and 1
	Oct 7	Speedboat Manta, gave help
1985	May 26	Speedboat, saved boat and 3
	July 6	Ingoldmells rescue boat, gave help
	7	Fishing boat in tow of Chapel rescue boat
		Ingoldmells rescue boat, gave help
	15	Speedboat, saved boat and 1

	Aug 1	Dinghy, gave help
	4	Sailboard, saved board and 1
	21	Airbed, saved 1
	22	Rubber dinghy, saved 1
	Sep 10	Rubber dinghy, saved dinghy
1986	Apr 18	Speedboat, gave help
	July 16	Rubber dinghy, saved dinghy
	Aug 5	Rubber dinghy, saved dinghy
	Sep 4	Speedboat Bosa Nova, gave help
	Oct 4	Cabin cruiser Mist, gave help

D-326 Michel Philippe Wolvers ILB

1987	June 1	Fishing boat, craft brought in – gave help
	July 31	Dinghy, saved dinghy and 2
1988	May 18	Fishing boat, gave help
	29	Fishing boat, craft brought in – gave help
	July 23	Dinghy, saved dinghy and 2
1989	Apr 19	Fishing vessel, escorted
	July 24	Powered boat, craft landed
	26	Rubber dinghy, saved dinghy
	27	Rubber dinghy, saved dinghy
		Rubber dinghy, saved dinghy and 3
		Safety boat, saved dinghy and 2
	28	Jet ski, stood by
	Aug 9	Rubber dinghy, saved dinghy and 1
		Swimmers, landed 2
	14	Rubber dinghy, saved dinghy
	20	Powered boat, landed 2, saved boat and 2
	24	Powered boat, saved boat and 7
	Sep 18	Sailboard, saved board and 1
1990	May 5	Fishing vessel, craft brought in
	June 19	Fishing vessel, craft brought in
	July 28	Person in sea, saved 1
	29	Sailboard, saved board and 1
	Aug 4	Sailing dinghy, escorted craft
	15	Sailboards, saved boards and 2
	Sep 9	Fishing vessel, gave help
1991	Apr 7	Sailboard, saved board and landed 1
	July 9	Jet ski, saved craft and 1
	29	Yacht, escorted

D-401 Banks' Staff Appeal IV Relief ILB

	Aug 10	Rubber dinghy, saved dinghy and 2
	23	Sailboard, escorted
	25	Swimmer, gave help
		Safety boat, craft brought in

D-326 Michel Philippe Wolvers ILB

1992	Apr 18	Sailboard, saved board and 1
	26	Fishing vessel, landed sick person
	June 27	Airbed, saved craft and 1
	July 17	Airbed, saved craft and 4
	27	Rubber dinghy, escorted
		Sailboard, saved board and 1
	28	Rubber dinghy, gave help
	Aug 13	Motor boat, saved boat and 2
	21	Cabin cruiser Bulvan Buccaneer, gave help
	Sep 15	Sailboard, saved board and 1
		Sailboard, escorted
1993	Apr 4	Power boat, craft brought in
	July 17	Sailing dinghy, saved dinghy and 3
	24	Rubber dinghy, gave help
	31	Sailboard, gave help

| | Aug 17 | Animal in water, gave help |
| | 19 | Rubber dinghy, saved craft |

D-460 Leicester Fox ILB

1994	July 24	Speedboat, escorted boat
	Aug 15	Rubber dinghy, escorted boat
1995	Apr 2	Rubber dinghy, craft brought in
	May 28	Rubber dinghy, two lives and boat saved
	July 4	Sailboard, one life and board saved
		Lifeguard, one person brought in
	7	Two rubber dinghies, two persons and two craft brought in
		Yacht, gave help
	15	Sailboard, landed 1 and saved board
	Aug 6	Speedboat Sink or Swim, two persons and craft brought in
	22	Rubber dinghy, escorted boat

D-378 Relief ILB

1996	June 5	Airbed, saved airbed and 1
	12	Rubber dinghy, saved craft and 1
		Airbeds, gave help
	July 4	Rubber dinghy, saved 2
	10	Rubber dinghy, saved craft and 2
	15	Swimmer, saved 1
	26	Rubber dinghy, saved 1
		Rubber dinghy, escorted craft
		Bather, gave help
	28	Rubber dinghy, saved craft and 1
		Rubber dinghy, escorted craft
	30	Bathers, saved 2
	31	Sailboard, board brought in
		Rubber dinghy, saved craft and 2
	Aug 7	Bathers, saved 2
	18	Two dinghies, saved 2
	22	Rubber dinghy, escorted craft
		Bathers, gave help
		Two swimmers, gave help
		Airbed, escorted airbed
	23	Rubber dinghy, saved craft and 1
	Sep 3	Missing boy, gave help

D-460 Leicester Fox ILB

	Dec 6	Survey vessel Jackie, two persons and craft brought in
1997	Jan 15	Motor boat Snoopy, saved craft
	July 4	Two swimmers, saved 2
	17	Jet ski, one person and jet ski brought in
		Bather, landed 1
	20	Speedboat, saved craft and 3
	25	Two rubber dinghies, saved two craft and 2
	27	Rubber dinghy, landed 2 and craft brought in
	30	Rubber dinghy, saved craft and 1
		Rubber dinghy, saved craft and 2
		Rubber dinghy, saved craft and 1
		Airbed, saved airbed and 2
		Rubber dinghy, saved craft and 2
	Aug 14	Bather, gave help
		Rubber dinghies, gave help
	20	Speedboat Nice and Easy, saved craft and 4
	21	Airbed, saved airbed and 1
		Three airbeds, saved three airbeds and 5
	Sep 1	Airbed and rubber dinghies, gave help
1998	Feb 8	Fishing vessel Our Irene, one person and craft brought in
	May 25	Inflatable dinghy, one person brought in
	June 1	Three airbeds, three people and three airbeds brought in
	7	Speedboat, two people and craft brought in

June 8	Fishing vessel Hannah Charlotte, gave help
July 24	Inflatable dinghies, saved dinghies
	Inflatable dinghy, saved craft and 1
	Swimmer, one person brought in
Aug 4	Inflatable dinghy, saved 1
	Inflatable dinghy, saved 3
	Inflatable dinghy, saved 2
5	Inflatable dinghy, saved craft
	Inflatable dinghies, saved craft
6	Two inflatable dinghies, saved craft
	Inflatable dinghy, escorted craft
	Inflatable dinghy, saved craft and 1
	Inflatable dinghy, gave help
7	Inflatable dinghy, gave help
	Inflatable dinghies, escorted craft
8	Speedboat Cheers, four people and craft brought in
11	Jet ski, one person and jet ski brought in
12	Bather, saved 1
15	Airbed, saved airbed and 2
	Inflatable dinghy, saved 2
	Two bathers, saved 2
19	Inflatable dinghy, saved 2
	Inflatable dinghy, saved craft and 2
Sep 10	Inflatable dinghy, saved 2
	Four missing children, gave help
Dec 27	Sailboard, saved board and 1

D-425 Strickson Relief ILB

1999	Apr 5	Airbed, saved 2
	6	Jet ski, saved craft
	June 4	Man in sea, saved 1
		Airbed, saved airbed and 1
	19	Inflatable dinghy, saved 1

D-460 Leicester Fox ILB

	Aug 5	Missing person, gave help
	13	Yacht saved craft and 7
	14	Speedboat, one person and craft brought in
	27	Inflatable dinghy, craft brought in
	29	Inflatable dinghy, craft brought in
		Man overboard from dinghy, saved 2
		Inflatable dinghy, gave help
	Sep 1	Inflatable dinghy, landed 2
		Inflatable dinghy, escorted craft
	5	Inflatable dinghy, escorted craft
2000	May 16	Dinghy, craft brought in
	Aug 1	Inflatable dinghies, gave help
		Inflatable dinghy, escorted casualty
	9	Inflatable dinghies, gave help
	10	Inflatable dinghy, saved 1
	11	Unidentified object in sea, gave help
	15	Dinghy, landed 3 and saved craft
	17	Dinghy, landed 2 and craft brought in
		Lifeguard in danger of drowning, landed 1
	19	Speedboat, two persons and craft brought in
	20	Swimmer, gave help
	27	Dinghy, saved craft and 3
	Sep 6	Inflatable dinghies, craft brought in
	24	Yacht Carpadium, gave help
2001	June 26	Yacht Wurzeler, two persons and craft brought in
	July 29	Speedboat, two persons and craft brought in
		Inflatable boat, landed 1 and craft brought in
		Inflatable dinghies, landed 5 and craft brought in
		Inflatable boat, landed 2
		Swimmers, landed 2

	Swimmers, landed 3
	Swimmers, landed 2
	Sick person on beach, gave help
	Inflatable dinghy, landed 2 and craft brought in
	Inflatable dinghy, landed 2 and craft brought in
	Inflatable dinghy, landed 3 and craft brought in
	Swimmers, landed 2
	Inflatable dinghy, landed 2 and craft brought in
	Jet ski, three persons and craft brought in
Aug 11	Kiteboard, saved craft and 1
15	Inflatable dinghies, escorted craft
16	Inflatable dinghy, gave help
20	Inflatable dinghy, saved craft and 3
Oct 17	Person cut off by the tide, landed 1
Nov 4	Fishing vessel, one person and craft brought in

D-425 Strickson Relief ILB

2002	June 18	Inflatable dinghies, two persons brought in
	21	Rowing boat, saved boat and 1
	22	Yacht Frantic, stood by
	July 7	Jet ski under tow of speedboat, escorted

D-573 Leicester Fox II ILB

	July 21	Three people from jet ski, landed 1, saved craft and 2
	24	Speedboat Impulse, one person and craft brought in
	26	Swimmer with inflatable, landed 1
		Inflatable dinghy, landed 2 and craft brought in
		Swimmer, saved 1
		Inflatable dinghy, landed 1 and craft brought in
		Swimmer with inflatable, landed 1
		Inflatable dinghy, saved craft and 2
		Inflatable dinghy, saved dinghy and 2
		Swimmer with inflatables, stood by
	28	Two inflatable dinghies, landed 2 and craft brought in
		Swimmer, saved 1
		Inflatable dinghy, landed 1 and craft brought in
		Airbed, saved craft and 2
		Various, gave help
	Aug 13	Inflatable dinghy, landed 3 and craft brought in
		Inflatable dinghy, two persons and craft brought in
		Lilo, escorted craft
		Persons overboard from dinghy, saved dinghy and 3
		Inflatable dinghy, two persons and craft brought in
		Swimmer with a rubber ring, person brought in
		Missing child, gave help
		Inflatable dinghy, landed 2 and craft brought in
		Inflatable dinghy, landed 1 and craft brought in
	19	Dinghy, craft brought in
	28	Swimmers, gave help
	29	Swimmers with inflatable, saved 2
		Jet ski, gave help
	Sep 17	Motor cruiser Pelican, two and craft brought in
	29	Fishing vessel Optimist, two and craft brought in

D-552 Global Marine Relief ILB

| 2003 | Jan 12 | Fishing boat Chalmari, one person and craft brought in |

D-573 Leicester Fox II ILB

	May 5	Jet ski, three persons and craft brought in
	June 14	Jet ski, one person and craft brought in
	15	Person in the water, assisted to save 1
	July 10	Swimmer, gave help
		Inflatable dinghy, escorted craft
	13	Inflatable dinghy, stood by

	July 18	Inflatable dinghy, landed 2 and craft brought in
		Inflatable dinghy, four craft brought in
	19	Inflatable dinghy, landed 2 and craft brought in
		Inflatable dinghies, craft brought in
		Inflatable dinghies, gave help
		Swimmers, gave help
		Inflatable dinghy, landed 1 and craft brought in
	22	Inflatable dinghy, landed 2 and craft brought in
		Missing child, gave help
	Aug 10	Inflatable dinghy, landed 2 and craft brought in
	13	Inflatable, landed 3 and craft brought in
		Inflatables, landed 6 and craft brought in
		Inflatable landed 2 and craft brought in
		Inflatable, landed 1 and craft brought in
		Swimmers, gave help
		More than 40 inflatables, craft brought in
	18	Inflatable dinghy, saved 2
2004	Apr 4	Inflatable dinghy, gave help

D-450 Anthony Relief ILB

	June 7	Inflatable dinghy, landed 1 and saved craft
	July 26	Inflatable dinghies, five persons and craft brought in
	28	Inflatable dinghies, escorted craft
	29	Person at risk, gave help
	Aug 2	Yacht Teniwa 2, landed 1
	6	Missing children, gave help – advice given
	16	Inflatable dinghy, saved dinghy and 2
	19	Person in danger of drowning, landed 1
	22	Jet ski, two persons and craft brought in
	26	Child missing, gave help – found child on beach
		Child missing, gave help – found child on beach
		Sailboard, saved board and 1
	29	Inflatable dinghy, saved 3
	Sep 26	Jet ski, one person brought in and saved craft
	30	Yacht Arawa, three persons brought in
	Oct 29	Kiteboard, one person and craft brought in

D-573 Leicester Fox II ILB

| 2005 | May 29 | Powered boat Four Winns, seven and craft brought in |

D-474 G. C. H. Fox Relief ILB

	June 23	Yacht Porpoise, two persons and craft brought in
	25	Person at risk, one person brought in
	July 13	Powered boat, two persons and craft brought in
	Aug 6	Yacht Florence 2, one person and craft brought in
	16	Powered boat Red Dwarf, four persons and craft brought in

	Aug 19	Jet ski, saved craft and 1
	23	Airbed, craft brought in
	28	Inflatable, landed 1
	30	Inflatables, craft brought in

D-573 Leicester Fox II ILB

	Sep 11	Diver support craft, four persons and craft brought in
	23	Kiteboarder, landed 1 and craft brought in
2006	Apr 17	Person in the sea, saved 1
	June 12	Kiteboard, one person and kiteboard brought in
	18	Kiteboard, gave help
		Airbed, airbed brought in
	July 19	Swimmers, gave help
	23	Missing child, one person brought in
		Inflatable dinghy, two persons and craft brought in
		Airbed, airbed brought in
	27	Swimmer, gave help
	30	Inflatable dinghy, two persons and craft brought in
		Inflatable toy, craft brought in
		Inflatable, one person brought in
		Inflatable, gave help
		Person in sea, one person and object brought in
	Aug 8	Catamaran, one person and craft brought in
		Missing child, gave help
	9	Airbed, one person and craft brought in
	20	Swimmer, saved 1
	Oct 14	Car, gave help
	Nov 26	Kiteboard, one person and kiteboard brought in
2007	Jan 1	Person cut off by the tide, landed 1
	May 18	Powered boat, saved craft and 2
	June 18	Inflatable dinghy, two persons and craft brought in
	28	Person at risk, gave help – administered first aid
	July 7	Jet ski, three persons and craft brought in
		Powered boat, four persons and craft brought in
	14	Powered boat, three persons brought in
	27	Inflatable dinghy, craft brought in
	Aug 1	Inflatable dinghy, escorted craft
	5	Swimmer, one person brought in
	14	Person at risk, gave help
	18	Swimmer, one person brought in
	25	Missing child, one child brought in
	30	Inflatable dinghy, one person and craft brought in
		Person in sea, stood by
	Oct 22	Yacht Pavana, gave help
2008	May 11	Jet ski, two persons and craft brought in

A team of launchers help push inshore lifeboat D-573 Leicester Fox II through the surf. (By courtesy of Skegness RNLI)

Manned by a crew of four, D-573 Leicester Fox II breaks through the surf off the beach. (By courtesy of Skegness RNLI)

5 • Personnel summary

Honorary Secretaries (since 1864)

William Everington	1864–1882
Charles Fred Grantham	1882–1922
Dr B. Sweeen	1922–1929
Ald G. G. Dunkley	1929–1933
H. E. Sparrow	1933–1947
Jack A. Palmer	1947–1949
Rev F. J. Wood	1949–1951
T. E. B. Kiss	1952–1955
Frank Janney	1955–1965
Frederick Neville Ball	1965–1985
Terence Smart	1985–1992
Barry A. Trevitt	1992
Joel Grunnill	1992–1994
Roland Broughton	1994–2.2000
Peter Newsome MBE	2.2000–4.2005
Alan Fisher	1.4.2005–

Coxswains

William Scupholm	1825–1830
Samuel Moody	1830–1871
Thomas Green	1871–11.1873
Joseph Moody	11.1873–1880
Thomas Smalley	1880–1900
John Smith Woody	1900–1908
Matthew Grunnill	1908–1932
George Perrin	1932–1947
Wilfred Perrin	1947–1965
Kenneth J. Holland BEM	1965–7.1985
(Joint Coxswain/Mechanic from 1969)	
Paul Martin*	7.1985–5.1989
Ron Chapman*	5–12.1989
Paul Martin*	1.1.1990–12.1999
John Irving*	12.1999–

Second Coxswains

Montague Grunnill	1908–1934
Harold Steele	1934–1951
Joel Grunnill	1951–1984
Ron Chapman	1984–12.1990
John Irving	1.1.1990–1999
Ray Chapman	1999–

Mechanics

Percy Grunnill	1932–1940
Wilfred Langford Grunnill	1940–1946
Percy Grunnill	1946–26.4.1968
Graham Jack Phillips (Asst Mech)	1965–2000
Ken Holland*	1969–1985
Paul Martin*	7.1985–5.1989
Ron Chapman*	5–12.1989
Paul Martin*	1.1.1990–12.1999
John Irving*	12.1999–

Head tractor drivers

Wilfred Grunnill
Bert Hides
Philip Holvey
John Foreman
Bert Burrows
John Griffiths
Brian Wright
Trevor Holland

* Joint Coxswain/Mechanic

Lifeboat Operations Manager Alan Fisher, previously station officer for the local Coastguard and a carpenter by trade. (Nicholas Leach)

Coxswain John Irving at the wheel of Lincolnshire Poacher, with Deputy Second Coxswain Richard Watson. (Nicholas Leach)